NATIONAL PARKS
BUCKET ADVENTURE
Passport, Stamp, and Tracker Logs
Included

"AND INTO THE FOREST I GO. TO LOSE MY MIND AND FIND MY SOUL." - JOHN MUIR

Scan the code to access
other Easy Beesy Travelers
travel related books

THIS TRAVEL JOURNAL
belongs to
Roger & Teresa

If found, please return to:

_____

_____

I have traveled these lands, documented my journey,
the memories are mine to live again in these pages.

U. S. NATIONAL PARKS
LISTED BY STATE

ALASKA
- ☐ DENALI
- ☐ GATES OF THE ARCTIC
- ☐ GLACIER BAY
- ☐ KATMAI
- ☐ KENAI FJORDS
- ☐ KOBUK VALLEY
- ☐ LAKE CLARK
- ☐ WRANGELL - ST. ELIAS

ARIZONA
- ☐ GRAND CANYON
- ☐ PETRIFIED FOREST
- ☐ SAGUARO

ARKANSAS
- ☑ HOT SPRINGS

CALIFORNIA
- ☐ CHANNEL ISLANDS
- ☐ DEATH VALLEY
- ☐ JOSHUA TREE
- ☐ KINGS CANYON
- ☐ LASSEN VOLCANIC
- ☐ PINNACLES
- ☐ REDWOOD
- ☐ SEQUOIA
- ☐ YOSEMITE

COLORADO
- ☐ BLACK CANYON OF GUNNISON
- ☐ GREAT SAND DUNES
- ☐ MESA VERDE
- ☐ ROCKY MOUNTAIN

FLORIDA
- ☐ BISCAYNE
- ☐ DRY TORTUGAS
- ☐ EVERGLADES

HAWAII
- ☐ HALEAKALA
- ☑ HAWAII VOLCANOES

INDIANA
- ☑ INDIANA DUNES

KENTUCKY
- ☑ MAMMOTH CAVE

MAINE
- ☐ ACADIA

MICHIGAN
- ☐ ISLE ROYALE

MINNESOTA
- ☐ VOYAGEURS

MISSOURI
- ☑ GATEWAY ARCH

MONTANNA
- ☐ GLACIER

NEVADA
- ☐ GREAT BASIN

NEW MEXICO
- ☐ CARLSBAD CAVERNS
- ☐ WHITE SANDS

NORTH DAKOTA
- ☑ THEODORE ROOSEVELT

OHIO
- ☑ CUYAHOGA VALLEY

OREGON
- ☐ CRATER LAKE

SOUTH CAROLINA
- ☐ CONGAREE

SOUTH DAKOTA
- ☑ BADLANDS
- ☐ WIND CAVE

TENNESSEE
- ☑ GREAT SMOKY MOUNTAINS

TEXAS
- ☐ BIG BEND
- ☐ GUADALUPE MOUNTAINS

UTAH
- ☐ ARCHES
- ☐ BRYCE CANYON
- ☐ CAPITOL REEF
- ☐ CANYONLANDS
- ☐ ZION

VIRGINIA
- ☐ SHENANDOAH

WASHINGTON
- ☑ MOUNT RAINIER
- ☐ NORTH CASCADES
- ☐ OLYMPIC

WEST VIRGINIA
- ☐ NEW RIVER GORGE

WYOMING
- ☐ GRAND TETON
- ☐ YELLOWSTONE

U.S. TERRITORIES
- ☐ AMERICAN SAMOA
- ☐ VIRGIN ISLANDS

"OF ALL THE PATHS YOU TAKE IN LIFE, MAKE SURE A FEW OF THEM ARE DIRT." – JOHN MUIR

Journal
SECTIONS

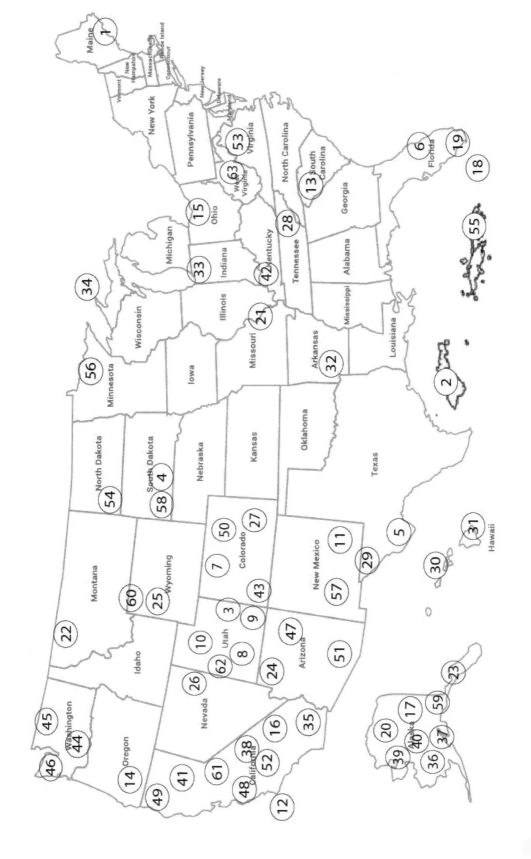

US National Parks and Territories

ON THE MAP

(1) Acadia
(2) American Samoa
(3) Arches
(4) Badlands
(5) Big Bend
(6) Biscayne
(7) Black Canyon of the Gunnison
(8) Bryce Canyon
(9) Canyonlands
(10) Capitol Reef
(11) Carlsbad Caverns
(12) Channel Islands
(13) Congaree
(14) Crater Lake

(15) Cuyahoga Valley
(16) Death Valley
(17) Denali
(18) Dry Tortugas
(19) Everglades
(20) Gates of the Arctic
(21) Gateway Arch
(22) Glacier
(23) Glacier Bay
(24) Grand Canyon
(25) Grand Teton
(26) Great Basin
(27) Great Sand Dunes
(28) Great Smoky Mountains

(29) Guadalupe Mountains
(30) Haleakalā
(31) Hawaiʻi Volcanoes
(32) Hot Springs
(33) Indiana Dunes
(34) Isle Royale
(35) Joshua Tree
(36) Katmai
(37) Kenai Fjords
(38) Kings Canyon
(39) Kobuk Valley
(40) Lake Clark
(41) Lassen Volcanic
(42) Mammoth Cave
(43) Mesa Verde

(44) Mount Rainier
(45) North Cascades
(46) Olympic
(47) Petrified Forest
(48) Pinnacles
(49) Redwood
(50) Rocky Mountain
(51) Saguaro
(52) Sequoia
(53) Shenandoah
(54) Theodore Roosevelt
(55) Virgin Islands
(56) Voyageurs
(57) White Sands
(58) Wind Cave

(59) Wrangell–St. Elias
(60) Yellowstone
(61) Yosemite
(62) Zion
(63) New River Gorge

My US National Park and Territories
BUCKET ADVENTURES LIST

Name	Date Established	Location	Date Visited
Acadia	2/26/1919	Maine	
American Samoa	10/31/1988	American Samoa	
Arches	11/12/1971	Utah	
Badlands	11/10/1978	South Dakota	
Big Bend	6/12/1944	Texas	
Biscayne	6/28/1980	Florida	
Black Canyon of the Gunnison	10/21/1999	Colorado	
Bryce Canyon	2/25/1928	Utah	
Canyonlands	9/12/1964	Utah	
Capitol Reef	12/18/1971	Utah	
Carlsbad Caverns	5/14/1930	New Mexico	
Channel Islands	3/5/1980	California	
Congaree	11/10/2003	South Carolina	
Crater Lake	5/22/1902	Oregon	
Cuyahoga Valley	10/11/2000	Ohio	
Death Valley	10/31/1994	California, Nevada	
Denali	2/26/1917	Alaska	
Dry Tortugas	10/26/1992	Florida	
Everglades	5/30/1934	Florida	
Gates of the Arctic	12/2/1980	Alaska	
Gateway Arch	2/22/2018	Missouri	
Glacier	5/11/1910	Montana	

"ITS NOT THE MOUNTAIN WE CONQUER, BUT OURSELVES." – SIR EDMUND HILLARY

Name	Date Established	Location	Date Visited
Glacier Bay	12/2/1980	Alaska	
Grand Canyon	2/26/1919	Arizona	
Grand Teton	2/26/1929	Wyoming	
Great Basin	10/27/1986	Nevada	
Great Sand Dunes	9/24/2004	Colorado	
Great Smoky	6/15/1934	North Carolina, Tennessee	
Guadalupe Mts	10/15/1966	Texas	
Haleakala	7/1/1961	Hawaii	
Hawaii Volcanoes	8/1/1916	Hawaii	
Hot Springs	3/4/1921	Arkansas	
Indiana Dunes	2/15/2019	Indiana	
Isle Royale	4/3/1940	Michigan	
Joshua Tree	10/31/1994	California	
Katmai	12/2/1980	Alaska	
Kenai Fjords	12/2/1980	Alaska	
Kings Canyon	3/4/1940	California	
Kobuk Valley	12/2/1980	Alaska	
Lake Clark	12/2/1980	Alaska	
Lassen Volcanic	8/9/1916	California	
Mammoth Cave	7/1/1941	Kentucky	
Mesa Verde	6/29/1906	Colorado	
Mount Rainier	3/2/1899	Washington	
New River Gorge	12/27/2020	West Virginia	
North Cascades	10/2/1968	Washington	
Olympic	6/29/1938	Washington	

"TO WALK IN NATURE IS TO WITNESS A THOUSAND MIRACLES." – MARY DAVIS

Name	Date Established	Location	Date Visited
Petrified Forest	12/9/1962	Arizona	
Pinnacles	1/10/2013	California	
Redwood	10/2/1968	California	
Rocky Mountain	1/26/1915	Colorado	
Saguaro	10/14/1994	Arizona	
Sequoia	9/25/1890	California	
Shenandoah	12/26/1935	Virginia	
Theodore Roosevelt	11/10/1978	North Dakota	
Virgin Islands	8/2/1956	U.S. Virgin Islands	
Voyageurs	4/8/1975	Minnesota	
White Sands	12/20/2019	New Mexico	
Wind Cave	1/9/1903	South Dakota	
Wrangell—St. Elias	12/2/1980	Alaska	
Yellowstone	3/1/1872	Wyoming, Montana, Idaho	
Yosemite	10/1/1890	California	
Zion	11/19/1919	Utah	

HOW TO USE THIS JOURNAL

The US National Park Bucket List Journal is for your adventure to be designed and documented by you with some basic prompts to help plan your National Park Excursion.

Track your park visit using the convenient Bucket List tracker at the front of the journal and watch your adventures grow.

Check your essentials necessary to make all park visits less stressful.

The 69 fill-in two-page prompted journal sets allow you to capture the most memorable parts of your bucket list goals. From rating your visit, experiences, and accommodations, the pages include checklists for the most important things you will need at each park and activities you want to experience. Extra park sets included for any adventures you want to repeat.

BONUS Pages:
Track in one place every step taken on a hike, the trail, the miles, the adventure, the fauna that catches your attention and the birds unique to the region you visit.

Each National Park's highlights are included in alphabetical order for you to see brief descriptions about each park and gain a small insight to what the park hosts.

Through the interactive scan codes, all you need to do is scan the park QR code with your phone or device and access the National Parks Foundation page and begin to plan your journey.

You don't have a device that allows for scanning the interactive codes? No problem. We've included quick access information for all the parks including, when available, the physical location of the park and the phone number to reach that specific parks information center.

PREPAREDNESS IS KEY

Priority
Bucket Adventures

PLACES TO VISIT

THINGS I WANT TO DO

FOODS TO TASTE

ACCOMMODATIONS

THE 10 ESSENTIALS PACKING LIST

No matter which National Park you visit, make sure you pack all ten essentials for your visit:

1. **Navigation** - Ensure you have a way to navigate the parks, other than a cellular device, such as GPS and physical maps. Be sure to familiarize yourself with how to read topographical and relief maps. Don't forget to pack your compass.
2. **Sun Protection** - Be sure to pack sunglasses, sun screen, hats, and appropriate clothing to protect against the sun's harsh UV rays.
3. **Insulation** - Be prepared for unpredictable weather, even in hot climates. Pack insulated clothing that protects and warms.
4. **Lighting** - Be sure to pack flashlights, lanterns and/or headlamps with plenty of extra batteries
5. **First Aid Supplies** - Be prepared for any emergency. Pre-made kits can be tailored to fit your trip and needs. An emergency guide will help with unfamiliar emergencies.
6. **Fire** - Pack waterproof matches and fire starters. Fire can be used both as an emergency signal and source of heat for cooking, purifying water, and staying warm. Be sure to check each park's rules regarding fire and fire safety.
7. **Repair kit** - Pack a basic repair kit that includes duct tape, a knife, scissors, multi-tool, and any trip specific tool.
8. **Nutrition** - Pack extra no cook items with good nutritional value in case of changes to plans. For outdoor activities, salty and easy to digest snacks like trail mix or granola work well.
9. **Water** - Pack plenty of water and then some.. Check your park before your trip for any bodies of water that you can collect water and treat using your water treatment supplies.
10. **Shelter** - Emergency shelter is important for survival situations. A lightweight tent, tarp, bivy sack, or space blanket are all easily portable options to pack.

BE PREPARED

NATIONAL PARK TRIP PLANNER:

City: _____ **State:** _____

Trip Start/End Date: _____

Anticipated Weather:

ACCOMMODATIONS: _____

PHONE: _____   PARK CELL RECEPTION ☐

PETS ALLOWED: ☐   PARK WIFI: ☐

SUPPLIES:

TO DO:

☐ LODGING RESERVATIONS
☐ PARK ENTRANCE PASS
☐ NATIONAL PARK/FED LANDS PASS
☐ TRIP PLAN FOR EMERGENCY
  CONTACT
☐ SAFETY LEADER: _____
☐ VEHICLE REGISTERED, IF
  REQUIRED
☐ DOWNLOAD NATIONAL PARK APP
☐ SAVED PARK FOR OFFLINE USE
☐ PACKED THE 10 ESSENTIALS
☐
☐
☐

PARK FEES

PARK ENTRANCE: _____
LODGING PER NIGHT: _____
VEHICLE REGISTRATION: _____
OTHER FEES: _____
_____
_____

ACTIVITY & PLACES TO VISIT ITINERARY

DATE/TIME	ACTIVITY	RESERVATIONS

OTHER NOTES:

NATIONAL PARK:

Overall Rating ☆ ☆ ☆ ☆ ☆

FAVORITE ACTIVITY:_____

FAVORITE TRAIL:_____

TOP WILDLIFE SIGHTS:_____

BEST SCENIC VIEWS_____

ACTIVITY ☆ ☆ ☆ ☆ ☆

LODGING ☆ ☆ ☆ ☆ ☆

FLORA & FAUNA ☆ ☆ ☆ ☆ ☆

CROWDS ☆ ☆ ☆ ☆ ☆

STARGAZING ☆ ☆ ☆ ☆ ☆

PASSPORT STAMP & MEMORABILIA

TO REMEMBER OR DO NEXT VISIT

ACTIVITY & RATING

_____	☆ ☆ ☆ ☆ ☆	_____	☆ ☆ ☆ ☆ ☆
_____	☆ ☆ ☆ ☆ ☆	_____	☆ ☆ ☆ ☆ ☆
_____	☆ ☆ ☆ ☆ ☆	_____	☆ ☆ ☆ ☆ ☆
_____	☆ ☆ ☆ ☆ ☆	_____	☆ ☆ ☆ ☆ ☆
_____	☆ ☆ ☆ ☆ ☆	_____	☆ ☆ ☆ ☆ ☆
_____	☆ ☆ ☆ ☆ ☆	_____	☆ ☆ ☆ ☆ ☆
_____	☆ ☆ ☆ ☆ ☆	_____	☆ ☆ ☆ ☆ ☆
	☆ ☆ ☆ ☆ ☆		☆ ☆ ☆ ☆ ☆

TRIP MEMORIES & OTHER NOTES:

NATIONAL PARK TRIP PLANNER:

City: **State:**

Anticipated Weather:

Trip Start/End Date: _____

ACCOMMODATIONS: _____

          PHONE: _____

     PETS ALLOWED: ☐

PARK CELL RECEPTION ☐

PARK WIFI: ☐

SUPPLIES:

PARK FEES

PARK ENTRANCE: _____

LODGING PER NIGHT: _____

VEHICLE REGISTRATION: _____

OTHER FEES: _____

_____

_____

TO DO:

☐ LODGING RESERVATIONS

☐ PARK ENTRANCE PASS

☐ NATIONAL PARK/FED LANDS PASS

☐ TRIP PLAN FOR EMERGENCY
    CONTACT

☐ SAFETY LEADER: _____

☐ VEHICLE REGISTERED, IF
    REQUIRED

☐ DOWNLOAD NATIONAL PARK APP

☐ SAVED PARK FOR OFFLINE USE

☐ PACKED THE 10 ESSENTIALS

☐

☐

☐

ACTIVITY & PLACES TO VISIT ITINERARY

DATE/TIME	ACTIVITY	RESERVATIONS

OTHER NOTES:

NATIONAL PARK:

Overall Rating ☆ ☆ ☆ ☆ ☆

FAVORITE ACTIVITY:_____

FAVORITE TRAIL:_____

TOP WILDLIFE SIGHTS:_____

BEST SCENIC VIEWS_____

ACTIVITY ☆ ☆ ☆ ☆ ☆

LODGING ☆ ☆ ☆ ☆ ☆

FLORA & FAUNA ☆ ☆ ☆ ☆ ☆

CROWDS ☆ ☆ ☆ ☆ ☆

STARGAZING ☆ ☆ ☆ ☆ ☆

PASSPORT STAMP & MEMORABILIA

TO REMEMBER OR DO NEXT VISIT

ACTIVITY & RATING

_____	☆ ☆ ☆ ☆ ☆	_____	☆ ☆ ☆ ☆ ☆
_____	☆ ☆ ☆ ☆ ☆	_____	☆ ☆ ☆ ☆ ☆
_____	☆ ☆ ☆ ☆ ☆	_____	☆ ☆ ☆ ☆ ☆
_____	☆ ☆ ☆ ☆ ☆	_____	☆ ☆ ☆ ☆ ☆
_____	☆ ☆ ☆ ☆ ☆	_____	☆ ☆ ☆ ☆ ☆
_____	☆ ☆ ☆ ☆ ☆	_____	☆ ☆ ☆ ☆ ☆
_____	☆ ☆ ☆ ☆ ☆	_____	☆ ☆ ☆ ☆ ☆
_____	☆ ☆ ☆ ☆ ☆	_____	☆ ☆ ☆ ☆ ☆

TRIP MEMORIES & OTHER NOTES:

NATIONAL PARK TRIP PLANNER:

City: _____ **State:** _____ **Anticipated Weather:**

Trip Start/End Date: _____

ACCOMMODATIONS: _____

PHONE: _____   PARK CELL RECEPTION ☐

PETS ALLOWED: ☐   PARK WIFI: ☐

SUPPLIES:

PARK FEES

PARK ENTRANCE: _____

LODGING PER NIGHT: _____

VEHICLE REGISTRATION: _____

OTHER FEES: _____

_____

_____

TO DO:

☐ LODGING RESERVATIONS

☐ PARK ENTRANCE PASS

☐ NATIONAL PARK/FED LANDS PASS

☐ TRIP PLAN FOR EMERGENCY CONTACT

☐ SAFETY LEADER: _____

☐ VEHICLE REGISTERED, IF REQUIRED

☐ DOWNLOAD NATIONAL PARK APP

☐ SAVED PARK FOR OFFLINE USE

☐ PACKED THE 10 ESSENTIALS

☐

☐

☐

ACTIVITY & PLACES TO VISIT ITINERARY

DATE/TIME	ACTIVITY	RESERVATIONS

OTHER NOTES:

NATIONAL PARK:

FAVORITE ACTIVITY: _____

FAVORITE TRAIL: _____

TOP WILDLIFE SIGHTS: _____

BEST SCENIC VIEWS _____

ACTIVITY ☆ ☆ ☆ ☆ ☆

LODGING ☆ ☆ ☆ ☆ ☆

FLORA & FAUNA ☆ ☆ ☆ ☆ ☆

CROWDS ☆ ☆ ☆ ☆ ☆

STARGAZING ☆ ☆ ☆ ☆ ☆

PASSPORT STAMP & MEMORABILIA

TO REMEMBER OR DO NEXT VISIT

ACTIVITY & RATING

_____	☆ ☆ ☆ ☆ ☆	_____	☆ ☆ ☆ ☆ ☆
_____	☆ ☆ ☆ ☆ ☆	_____	☆ ☆ ☆ ☆ ☆
_____	☆ ☆ ☆ ☆ ☆	_____	☆ ☆ ☆ ☆ ☆
_____	☆ ☆ ☆ ☆ ☆	_____	☆ ☆ ☆ ☆ ☆
_____	☆ ☆ ☆ ☆ ☆	_____	☆ ☆ ☆ ☆ ☆
_____	☆ ☆ ☆ ☆ ☆	_____	☆ ☆ ☆ ☆ ☆
_____	☆ ☆ ☆ ☆ ☆	_____	☆ ☆ ☆ ☆ ☆
	☆ ☆ ☆ ☆ ☆		☆ ☆ ☆ ☆ ☆

TRIP MEMORIES & OTHER NOTES:

NATIONAL PARK TRIP PLANNER:

City: **State:**   **Anticipated Weather:**

Trip Start/End Date:_____

ACCOMMODATIONS: _____

PHONE: _____   PARK CELL RECEPTION ☐

PETS ALLOWED: ☐   PARK WIFI: ☐

SUPPLIES:

PARK FEES

PARK ENTRANCE:_____

LODGING PER NIGHT:_____

VEHICLE REGISTRATION: _____

OTHER FEES:_____

_____

_____

TO DO:

☐ LODGING RESERVATIONS

☐ PARK ENTRANCE PASS

☐ NATIONAL PARK/FED LANDS PASS

☐ TRIP PLAN FOR EMERGENCY
CONTACT

☐ SAFETY LEADER: _____

☐ VEHICLE REGISTERED, IF
REQUIRED

☐ DOWNLOAD NATIONAL PARK APP

☐ SAVED PARK FOR OFFLINE USE

☐ PACKED THE 10 ESSENTIALS

☐

☐

☐

ACTIVITY & PLACES TO VISIT ITINERARY

DATE/TIME	ACTIVITY	RESERVATIONS

OTHER NOTES:

NATIONAL PARK:

Overall Rating ☆ ☆ ☆ ☆ ☆

FAVORITE ACTIVITY:_____

FAVORITE TRAIL:_____

TOP WILDLIFE SIGHTS:_____

BEST SCENIC VIEWS_____

ACTIVITY ☆ ☆ ☆ ☆ ☆

LODGING ☆ ☆ ☆ ☆ ☆

FLORA & FAUNA ☆ ☆ ☆ ☆ ☆

CROWDS ☆ ☆ ☆ ☆ ☆

STARGAZING ☆ ☆ ☆ ☆ ☆

PASSPORT STAMP & MEMORABILIA

TO REMEMBER OR DO NEXT VISIT

ACTIVITY & RATING

_____	☆ ☆ ☆ ☆ ☆	_____	☆ ☆ ☆ ☆ ☆
_____	☆ ☆ ☆ ☆ ☆	_____	☆ ☆ ☆ ☆ ☆
_____	☆ ☆ ☆ ☆ ☆	_____	☆ ☆ ☆ ☆ ☆
_____	☆ ☆ ☆ ☆ ☆	_____	☆ ☆ ☆ ☆ ☆
_____	☆ ☆ ☆ ☆ ☆	_____	☆ ☆ ☆ ☆ ☆
_____	☆ ☆ ☆ ☆ ☆	_____	☆ ☆ ☆ ☆ ☆
_____	☆ ☆ ☆ ☆ ☆	_____	☆ ☆ ☆ ☆ ☆
	☆ ☆ ☆ ☆ ☆		☆ ☆ ☆ ☆ ☆

TRIP MEMORIES & OTHER NOTES:

NATIONAL PARK TRIP PLANNER:

City: **State:**   **Anticipated Weather:**

Trip Start/End Date:_____

ACCOMMODATIONS: _____

PHONE: _____   PARK CELL RECEPTION ☐

PETS ALLOWED: ☐   PARK WIFI: ☐

SUPPLIES:

TO DO:

- ☐ LODGING RESERVATIONS
- ☐ PARK ENTRANCE PASS
- ☐ NATIONAL PARK/FED LANDS PASS
- ☐ TRIP PLAN FOR EMERGENCY CONTACT
- ☐ SAFETY LEADER: _____
- ☐ VEHICLE REGISTERED, IF REQUIRED
- ☐ DOWNLOAD NATIONAL PARK APP
- ☐ SAVED PARK FOR OFFLINE USE
- ☐ PACKED THE 10 ESSENTIALS
- ☐
- ☐
- ☐

PARK FEES

PARK ENTRANCE:_____

LODGING PER NIGHT:_____

VEHICLE REGISTRATION: _____

OTHER FEES:_____

_____

_____

ACTIVITY & PLACES TO VISIT ITINERARY

DATE/TIME	ACTIVITY	RESERVATIONS

OTHER NOTES:

NATIONAL PARK:

Overall Rating ☆ ☆ ☆ ☆ ☆

FAVORITE ACTIVITY:_____

FAVORITE TRAIL:_____

TOP WILDLIFE SIGHTS:_____

BEST SCENIC VIEWS_____

ACTIVITY ☆ ☆ ☆ ☆ ☆

LODGING ☆ ☆ ☆ ☆ ☆

FLORA & FAUNA ☆ ☆ ☆ ☆ ☆

CROWDS ☆ ☆ ☆ ☆ ☆

STARGAZING ☆ ☆ ☆ ☆ ☆

PASSPORT STAMP & MEMORABILIA

TO REMEMBER OR DO NEXT VISIT

ACTIVITY & RATING

_____	☆ ☆ ☆ ☆ ☆	_____	☆ ☆ ☆ ☆ ☆
_____	☆ ☆ ☆ ☆ ☆	_____	☆ ☆ ☆ ☆ ☆
_____	☆ ☆ ☆ ☆ ☆	_____	☆ ☆ ☆ ☆ ☆
_____	☆ ☆ ☆ ☆ ☆	_____	☆ ☆ ☆ ☆ ☆
_____	☆ ☆ ☆ ☆ ☆	_____	☆ ☆ ☆ ☆ ☆
_____	☆ ☆ ☆ ☆ ☆	_____	☆ ☆ ☆ ☆ ☆
_____	☆ ☆ ☆ ☆ ☆	_____	☆ ☆ ☆ ☆ ☆
_____	☆ ☆ ☆ ☆ ☆	_____	☆ ☆ ☆ ☆ ☆

TRIP MEMORIES & OTHER NOTES:

National Park Trip Planner:

City: **State:**

Trip Start/End Date: _____

Anticipated Weather:

ACCOMMODATIONS: _____

PHONE: _____   PARK CELL RECEPTION ☐

PETS ALLOWED: ☐   PARK WIFI: ☐

SUPPLIES:

TO DO:
- ☐ LODGING RESERVATIONS
- ☐ PARK ENTRANCE PASS
- ☐ NATIONAL PARK/FED LANDS PASS
- ☐ TRIP PLAN FOR EMERGENCY CONTACT
- ☐ SAFETY LEADER: _____
- ☐ VEHICLE REGISTERED, IF REQUIRED
- ☐ DOWNLOAD NATIONAL PARK APP
- ☐ SAVED PARK FOR OFFLINE USE
- ☐ PACKED THE 10 ESSENTIALS
- ☐
- ☐
- ☐

PARK FEES

PARK ENTRANCE: _____

LODGING PER NIGHT: _____

VEHICLE REGISTRATION: _____

OTHER FEES: _____

_____

_____

ACTIVITY & PLACES TO VISIT ITINERARY

DATE/TIME	ACTIVITY	RESERVATIONS

OTHER NOTES:

NATIONAL PARK:

Overall Rating ☆ ☆ ☆ ☆ ☆

FAVORITE ACTIVITY:_____

FAVORITE TRAIL:_____

TOP WILDLIFE SIGHTS:_____

BEST SCENIC VIEWS_____

ACTIVITY ☆ ☆ ☆ ☆ ☆

LODGING ☆ ☆ ☆ ☆ ☆

FLORA & FAUNA ☆ ☆ ☆ ☆ ☆

CROWDS ☆ ☆ ☆ ☆ ☆

STARGAZING ☆ ☆ ☆ ☆ ☆

PASSPORT STAMP & MEMORABILIA

TO REMEMBER OR DO NEXT VISIT

ACTIVITY & RATING

_____	☆ ☆ ☆ ☆ ☆	_____	☆ ☆ ☆ ☆ ☆
_____	☆ ☆ ☆ ☆ ☆	_____	☆ ☆ ☆ ☆ ☆
_____	☆ ☆ ☆ ☆ ☆	_____	☆ ☆ ☆ ☆ ☆
_____	☆ ☆ ☆ ☆ ☆	_____	☆ ☆ ☆ ☆ ☆
_____	☆ ☆ ☆ ☆ ☆	_____	☆ ☆ ☆ ☆ ☆
_____	☆ ☆ ☆ ☆ ☆	_____	☆ ☆ ☆ ☆ ☆
_____	☆ ☆ ☆ ☆ ☆	_____	☆ ☆ ☆ ☆ ☆
	☆ ☆ ☆ ☆ ☆		☆ ☆ ☆ ☆ ☆

TRIP MEMORIES & OTHER NOTES:

NATIONAL PARK TRIP PLANNER:

City: _____ **State:** _____

Trip Start/End Date: _____

Anticipated Weather:

ACCOMMODATIONS: _____

PHONE: _____   PARK CELL RECEPTION ☐

PETS ALLOWED: ☐   PARK WIFI: ☐

SUPPLIES:

PARK FEES

PARK ENTRANCE: _____

LODGING PER NIGHT: _____

VEHICLE REGISTRATION: _____

OTHER FEES: _____

_____

_____

TO DO:

☐ LODGING RESERVATIONS
☐ PARK ENTRANCE PASS
☐ NATIONAL PARK/FED LANDS PASS
☐ TRIP PLAN FOR EMERGENCY
   CONTACT
☐ SAFETY LEADER: _____
☐ VEHICLE REGISTERED, IF
   REQUIRED
☐ DOWNLOAD NATIONAL PARK APP
☐ SAVED PARK FOR OFFLINE USE
☐ PACKED THE 10 ESSENTIALS
☐
☐
☐

ACTIVITY & PLACES TO VISIT ITINERARY

DATE/TIME	ACTIVITY	RESERVATIONS

OTHER NOTES:

NATIONAL PARK:

Overall Rating ☆ ☆ ☆ ☆ ☆

FAVORITE ACTIVITY:_____

FAVORITE TRAIL:_____

TOP WILDLIFE SIGHTS:_____

BEST SCENIC VIEWS_____

ACTIVITY ☆ ☆ ☆ ☆ ☆

LODGING ☆ ☆ ☆ ☆ ☆

FLORA & FAUNA ☆ ☆ ☆ ☆ ☆

CROWDS ☆ ☆ ☆ ☆ ☆

STARGAZING ☆ ☆ ☆ ☆ ☆

PASSPORT STAMP & MEMORABILIA

TO REMEMBER OR DO NEXT VISIT

ACTIVITY & RATING

_____	☆ ☆ ☆ ☆ ☆	_____	☆ ☆ ☆ ☆ ☆
_____	☆ ☆ ☆ ☆ ☆	_____	☆ ☆ ☆ ☆ ☆
_____	☆ ☆ ☆ ☆ ☆	_____	☆ ☆ ☆ ☆ ☆
_____	☆ ☆ ☆ ☆ ☆	_____	☆ ☆ ☆ ☆ ☆
_____	☆ ☆ ☆ ☆ ☆	_____	☆ ☆ ☆ ☆ ☆
_____	☆ ☆ ☆ ☆ ☆	_____	☆ ☆ ☆ ☆ ☆
_____	☆ ☆ ☆ ☆ ☆	_____	☆ ☆ ☆ ☆ ☆
	☆ ☆ ☆ ☆ ☆		☆ ☆ ☆ ☆ ☆

TRIP MEMORIES & OTHER NOTES:

NATIONAL PARK TRIP PLANNER:

City: **State:**   **Anticipated Weather:**

Trip Start/End Date: _____

ACCOMMODATIONS: _____

                PHONE: _____   PARK CELL RECEPTION ☐

        PETS ALLOWED: ☐   PARK WIFI: ☐

SUPPLIES:

TO DO:

☐ LODGING RESERVATIONS
☐ PARK ENTRANCE PASS
☐ NATIONAL PARK/FED LANDS PASS
☐ TRIP PLAN FOR EMERGENCY
    CONTACT
☐ SAFETY LEADER: _____
☐ VEHICLE REGISTERED, IF
    REQUIRED
☐ DOWNLOAD NATIONAL PARK APP
☐ SAVED PARK FOR OFFLINE USE
☐ PACKED THE 10 ESSENTIALS
☐
☐
☐

PARK FEES

PARK ENTRANCE:_____
LODGING PER NIGHT:_____
VEHICLE REGISTRATION: _____
OTHER FEES:_____
_____
_____

ACTIVITY & PLACES TO VISIT ITINERARY

DATE/TIME	ACTIVITY	RESERVATIONS

OTHER NOTES:

NATIONAL PARK:

Overall Rating ☆ ☆ ☆ ☆ ☆

FAVORITE ACTIVITY: _____

FAVORITE TRAIL: _____

TOP WILDLIFE SIGHTS: _____

BEST SCENIC VIEWS _____

ACTIVITY ☆ ☆ ☆ ☆ ☆

LODGING ☆ ☆ ☆ ☆ ☆

FLORA & FAUNA ☆ ☆ ☆ ☆ ☆

CROWDS ☆ ☆ ☆ ☆ ☆

STARGAZING ☆ ☆ ☆ ☆ ☆

PASSPORT STAMP & MEMORABILIA

TO REMEMBER OR DO NEXT VISIT

ACTIVITY & RATING

_____	☆ ☆ ☆ ☆ ☆	_____	☆ ☆ ☆ ☆ ☆
_____	☆ ☆ ☆ ☆ ☆	_____	☆ ☆ ☆ ☆ ☆
_____	☆ ☆ ☆ ☆ ☆	_____	☆ ☆ ☆ ☆ ☆
_____	☆ ☆ ☆ ☆ ☆	_____	☆ ☆ ☆ ☆ ☆
_____	☆ ☆ ☆ ☆ ☆	_____	☆ ☆ ☆ ☆ ☆
_____	☆ ☆ ☆ ☆ ☆	_____	☆ ☆ ☆ ☆ ☆
_____	☆ ☆ ☆ ☆ ☆	_____	☆ ☆ ☆ ☆ ☆
	☆ ☆ ☆ ☆ ☆		☆ ☆ ☆ ☆ ☆

TRIP MEMORIES & OTHER NOTES:

NATIONAL PARK TRIP PLANNER:

City: _____ **State:** _____ **Anticipated Weather:**

Trip Start/End Date: _____

ACCOMMODATIONS: _____

PHONE: _____ PARK CELL RECEPTION ☐

PETS ALLOWED: ☐ PARK WIFI: ☐

SUPPLIES:

TO DO:

☐ LODGING RESERVATIONS

☐ PARK ENTRANCE PASS

☐ NATIONAL PARK/FED LANDS PASS

☐ TRIP PLAN FOR EMERGENCY
  CONTACT

☐ SAFETY LEADER: _____

☐ VEHICLE REGISTERED, IF
  REQUIRED

☐ DOWNLOAD NATIONAL PARK APP

☐ SAVED PARK FOR OFFLINE USE

☐ PACKED THE 10 ESSENTIALS

☐

☐

☐

PARK FEES

PARK ENTRANCE: _____

LODGING PER NIGHT: _____

VEHICLE REGISTRATION: _____

OTHER FEES: _____

_____

_____

ACTIVITY & PLACES TO VISIT ITINERARY

DATE/TIME	ACTIVITY	RESERVATIONS

OTHER NOTES:

NATIONAL PARK:

Overall Rating ☆ ☆ ☆ ☆ ☆

FAVORITE ACTIVITY:_____

FAVORITE TRAIL:_____

TOP WILDLIFE SIGHTS:_____

BEST SCENIC VIEWS_____

ACTIVITY ☆ ☆ ☆ ☆ ☆

LODGING ☆ ☆ ☆ ☆ ☆

FLORA & FAUNA ☆ ☆ ☆ ☆ ☆

CROWDS ☆ ☆ ☆ ☆ ☆

STARGAZING ☆ ☆ ☆ ☆ ☆

PASSPORT STAMP & MEMORABILIA

TO REMEMBER OR DO NEXT VISIT

ACTIVITY & RATING

_____	☆ ☆ ☆ ☆ ☆	_____	☆ ☆ ☆ ☆ ☆
_____	☆ ☆ ☆ ☆ ☆	_____	☆ ☆ ☆ ☆ ☆
_____	☆ ☆ ☆ ☆ ☆	_____	☆ ☆ ☆ ☆ ☆
_____	☆ ☆ ☆ ☆ ☆	_____	☆ ☆ ☆ ☆ ☆
_____	☆ ☆ ☆ ☆ ☆	_____	☆ ☆ ☆ ☆ ☆
_____	☆ ☆ ☆ ☆ ☆	_____	☆ ☆ ☆ ☆ ☆
_____	☆ ☆ ☆ ☆ ☆	_____	☆ ☆ ☆ ☆ ☆
	☆ ☆ ☆ ☆ ☆		☆ ☆ ☆ ☆ ☆

TRIP MEMORIES & OTHER NOTES:

National Park Trip Planner:

City: _____ **State:** _____

Trip Start/End Date: _____

Anticipated Weather:

ACCOMMODATIONS: _____

PHONE: _____   PARK CELL RECEPTION ☐

PETS ALLOWED: ☐   PARK WIFI: ☐

SUPPLIES:

TO DO:

☐ LODGING RESERVATIONS
☐ PARK ENTRANCE PASS
☐ NATIONAL PARK/FED LANDS PASS
☐ TRIP PLAN FOR EMERGENCY
  CONTACT
☐ SAFETY LEADER: _____
☐ VEHICLE REGISTERED, IF
  REQUIRED
☐ DOWNLOAD NATIONAL PARK APP
☐ SAVED PARK FOR OFFLINE USE
☐ PACKED THE 10 ESSENTIALS
☐
☐
☐

PARK FEES

PARK ENTRANCE: _____

LODGING PER NIGHT: _____

VEHICLE REGISTRATION: _____

OTHER FEES: _____

_____

_____

ACTIVITY & PLACES TO VISIT ITINERARY

DATE/TIME	ACTIVITY	RESERVATIONS

OTHER NOTES:

NATIONAL PARK:

Overall Rating ☆ ☆ ☆ ☆ ☆

FAVORITE ACTIVITY:_____

FAVORITE TRAIL:_____

TOP WILDLIFE SIGHTS:_____

BEST SCENIC VIEWS_____

ACTIVITY ☆ ☆ ☆ ☆ ☆

LODGING ☆ ☆ ☆ ☆ ☆

FLORA & FAUNA ☆ ☆ ☆ ☆ ☆

CROWDS ☆ ☆ ☆ ☆ ☆

STARGAZING ☆ ☆ ☆ ☆ ☆

PASSPORT STAMP & MEMORABILIA

TO REMEMBER OR DO NEXT VISIT

ACTIVITY & RATING

_____	☆ ☆ ☆ ☆ ☆	_____	☆ ☆ ☆ ☆ ☆
_____	☆ ☆ ☆ ☆ ☆	_____	☆ ☆ ☆ ☆ ☆
_____	☆ ☆ ☆ ☆ ☆	_____	☆ ☆ ☆ ☆ ☆
_____	☆ ☆ ☆ ☆ ☆	_____	☆ ☆ ☆ ☆ ☆
_____	☆ ☆ ☆ ☆ ☆	_____	☆ ☆ ☆ ☆ ☆
_____	☆ ☆ ☆ ☆ ☆	_____	☆ ☆ ☆ ☆ ☆
_____	☆ ☆ ☆ ☆ ☆	_____	☆ ☆ ☆ ☆ ☆
	☆ ☆ ☆ ☆ ☆		☆ ☆ ☆ ☆ ☆

TRIP MEMORIES & OTHER NOTES:

National Park Trip Planner:

City: **State:** **Anticipated Weather:**

Trip Start/End Date:_____

ACCOMMODATIONS: _____

PHONE: _____ PARK CELL RECEPTION ☐

PETS ALLOWED: ☐ PARK WIFI: ☐

SUPPLIES:

TO DO:
- ☐ LODGING RESERVATIONS
- ☐ PARK ENTRANCE PASS
- ☐ NATIONAL PARK/FED LANDS PASS
- ☐ TRIP PLAN FOR EMERGENCY CONTACT
- ☐ SAFETY LEADER: _____
- ☐ VEHICLE REGISTERED, IF REQUIRED
- ☐ DOWNLOAD NATIONAL PARK APP
- ☐ SAVED PARK FOR OFFLINE USE
- ☐ PACKED THE 10 ESSENTIALS
- ☐
- ☐
- ☐

PARK FEES

PARK ENTRANCE:_____

LODGING PER NIGHT:_____

VEHICLE REGISTRATION: _____

OTHER FEES:_____

_____

_____

ACTIVITY & PLACES TO VISIT ITINERARY

DATE/TIME	ACTIVITY	RESERVATIONS

OTHER NOTES:

NATIONAL PARK:

Overall Rating ☆ ☆ ☆ ☆ ☆

FAVORITE ACTIVITY:_____

FAVORITE TRAIL:_____

TOP WILDLIFE SIGHTS:_____

BEST SCENIC VIEWS_____

ACTIVITY ☆ ☆ ☆ ☆ ☆

LODGING ☆ ☆ ☆ ☆ ☆

FLORA & FAUNA ☆ ☆ ☆ ☆ ☆

CROWDS ☆ ☆ ☆ ☆ ☆

STARGAZING ☆ ☆ ☆ ☆ ☆

PASSPORT STAMP & MEMORABILIA

TO REMEMBER OR DO NEXT VISIT

ACTIVITY & RATING

_____	☆ ☆ ☆ ☆ ☆	_____	☆ ☆ ☆ ☆ ☆
_____	☆ ☆ ☆ ☆ ☆	_____	☆ ☆ ☆ ☆ ☆
_____	☆ ☆ ☆ ☆ ☆	_____	☆ ☆ ☆ ☆ ☆
_____	☆ ☆ ☆ ☆ ☆	_____	☆ ☆ ☆ ☆ ☆
_____	☆ ☆ ☆ ☆ ☆	_____	☆ ☆ ☆ ☆ ☆
_____	☆ ☆ ☆ ☆ ☆	_____	☆ ☆ ☆ ☆ ☆
_____	☆ ☆ ☆ ☆ ☆	_____	☆ ☆ ☆ ☆ ☆
	☆ ☆ ☆ ☆ ☆		☆ ☆ ☆ ☆ ☆

TRIP MEMORIES & OTHER NOTES:

NATIONAL PARK TRIP PLANNER:

City: _____ **State:** _____

Trip Start/End Date: _____

Anticipated Weather:

ACCOMMODATIONS: _____

PHONE: _____ PARK CELL RECEPTION ☐

PETS ALLOWED: ☐ PARK WIFI: ☐

SUPPLIES:

PARK FEES

PARK ENTRANCE: _____

LODGING PER NIGHT: _____

VEHICLE REGISTRATION: _____

OTHER FEES: _____

_____

_____

TO DO:

☐ LODGING RESERVATIONS

☐ PARK ENTRANCE PASS

☐ NATIONAL PARK/FED LANDS PASS

☐ TRIP PLAN FOR EMERGENCY
CONTACT

☐ SAFETY LEADER: _____

☐ VEHICLE REGISTERED, IF
REQUIRED

☐ DOWNLOAD NATIONAL PARK APP

☐ SAVED PARK FOR OFFLINE USE

☐ PACKED THE 10 ESSENTIALS

☐

☐

☐

ACTIVITY & PLACES TO VISIT ITINERARY

DATE/TIME	ACTIVITY	RESERVATIONS

OTHER NOTES:

NATIONAL PARK:

Overall Rating ☆ ☆ ☆ ☆ ☆

FAVORITE ACTIVITY:_____

FAVORITE TRAIL:_____

TOP WILDLIFE SIGHTS:_____

BEST SCENIC VIEWS_____

ACTIVITY ☆ ☆ ☆ ☆ ☆

LODGING ☆ ☆ ☆ ☆ ☆

FLORA & FAUNA ☆ ☆ ☆ ☆ ☆

CROWDS ☆ ☆ ☆ ☆ ☆

STARGAZING ☆ ☆ ☆ ☆ ☆

PASSPORT STAMP & MEMORABILIA

TO REMEMBER OR DO NEXT VISIT

ACTIVITY & RATING

_____ ☆ ☆ ☆ ☆ ☆	_____ ☆ ☆ ☆ ☆ ☆	
_____ ☆ ☆ ☆ ☆ ☆	_____ ☆ ☆ ☆ ☆ ☆	
_____ ☆ ☆ ☆ ☆ ☆	_____ ☆ ☆ ☆ ☆ ☆	
_____ ☆ ☆ ☆ ☆ ☆	_____ ☆ ☆ ☆ ☆ ☆	
_____ ☆ ☆ ☆ ☆ ☆	_____ ☆ ☆ ☆ ☆ ☆	
_____ ☆ ☆ ☆ ☆ ☆	_____ ☆ ☆ ☆ ☆ ☆	
_____ ☆ ☆ ☆ ☆ ☆	_____ ☆ ☆ ☆ ☆ ☆	
☆ ☆ ☆ ☆ ☆	☆ ☆ ☆ ☆ ☆	

TRIP MEMORIES & OTHER NOTES:

NATIONAL PARK TRIP PLANNER:

City: _____ **State:** _____

Anticipated Weather:

Trip Start/End Date: _____

ACCOMMODATIONS: _____

PHONE: _____   PARK CELL RECEPTION ☐

PETS ALLOWED: ☐   PARK WIFI: ☐

SUPPLIES:

TO DO:

☐ LODGING RESERVATIONS
☐ PARK ENTRANCE PASS
☐ NATIONAL PARK/FED LANDS PASS
☐ TRIP PLAN FOR EMERGENCY
   CONTACT
☐ SAFETY LEADER: _____
☐ VEHICLE REGISTERED, IF
   REQUIRED
☐ DOWNLOAD NATIONAL PARK APP
☐ SAVED PARK FOR OFFLINE USE
☐ PACKED THE 10 ESSENTIALS
☐
☐
☐

PARK FEES

PARK ENTRANCE: _____

LODGING PER NIGHT: _____

VEHICLE REGISTRATION: _____

OTHER FEES: _____

_____

_____

ACTIVITY & PLACES TO VISIT ITINERARY

DATE/TIME	ACTIVITY	RESERVATIONS

OTHER NOTES:

NATIONAL PARK:

Overall Rating ☆ ☆ ☆ ☆ ☆

FAVORITE ACTIVITY:_____

FAVORITE TRAIL:_____

TOP WILDLIFE SIGHTS:_____

BEST SCENIC VIEWS_____

ACTIVITY ☆ ☆ ☆ ☆ ☆

LODGING ☆ ☆ ☆ ☆ ☆

FLORA & FAUNA ☆ ☆ ☆ ☆ ☆

CROWDS ☆ ☆ ☆ ☆ ☆

STARGAZING ☆ ☆ ☆ ☆ ☆

PASSPORT STAMP & MEMORABILIA

TO REMEMBER OR DO NEXT VISIT

ACTIVITY & RATING

_____	☆ ☆ ☆ ☆ ☆	_____	☆ ☆ ☆ ☆ ☆
_____	☆ ☆ ☆ ☆ ☆	_____	☆ ☆ ☆ ☆ ☆
_____	☆ ☆ ☆ ☆ ☆	_____	☆ ☆ ☆ ☆ ☆
_____	☆ ☆ ☆ ☆ ☆	_____	☆ ☆ ☆ ☆ ☆
_____	☆ ☆ ☆ ☆ ☆	_____	☆ ☆ ☆ ☆ ☆
_____	☆ ☆ ☆ ☆ ☆	_____	☆ ☆ ☆ ☆ ☆
_____	☆ ☆ ☆ ☆ ☆	_____	☆ ☆ ☆ ☆ ☆
_____	☆ ☆ ☆ ☆ ☆	_____	☆ ☆ ☆ ☆ ☆

TRIP MEMORIES & OTHER NOTES:

NATIONAL PARK TRIP PLANNER:

City: _____ **State:** _____

Trip Start/End Date: _____

Anticipated Weather:

ACCOMMODATIONS: _____

PHONE: _____

PETS ALLOWED: ☐

PARK CELL RECEPTION ☐

PARK WIFI: ☐

SUPPLIES:

TO DO:

☐ LODGING RESERVATIONS
☐ PARK ENTRANCE PASS
☐ NATIONAL PARK/FED LANDS PASS
☐ TRIP PLAN FOR EMERGENCY CONTACT
☐ SAFETY LEADER: _____
☐ VEHICLE REGISTERED, IF REQUIRED
☐ DOWNLOAD NATIONAL PARK APP
☐ SAVED PARK FOR OFFLINE USE
☐ PACKED THE 10 ESSENTIALS
☐
☐
☐

PARK FEES

PARK ENTRANCE: _____

LODGING PER NIGHT: _____

VEHICLE REGISTRATION: _____

OTHER FEES: _____

_____

_____

ACTIVITY & PLACES TO VISIT ITINERARY

DATE/TIME	ACTIVITY	RESERVATIONS

OTHER NOTES:

NATIONAL PARK:

Overall Rating ☆ ☆ ☆ ☆ ☆

FAVORITE ACTIVITY:_____

FAVORITE TRAIL:_____

TOP WILDLIFE SIGHTS:_____

BEST SCENIC VIEWS_____

ACTIVITY ☆ ☆ ☆ ☆ ☆

LODGING ☆ ☆ ☆ ☆ ☆

FLORA & FAUNA ☆ ☆ ☆ ☆ ☆

CROWDS ☆ ☆ ☆ ☆ ☆

STARGAZING ☆ ☆ ☆ ☆ ☆

PASSPORT STAMP & MEMORABILIA

TO REMEMBER OR DO NEXT VISIT

ACTIVITY & RATING

_____	☆ ☆ ☆ ☆ ☆	_____	☆ ☆ ☆ ☆ ☆
_____	☆ ☆ ☆ ☆ ☆	_____	☆ ☆ ☆ ☆ ☆
_____	☆ ☆ ☆ ☆ ☆	_____	☆ ☆ ☆ ☆ ☆
_____	☆ ☆ ☆ ☆ ☆	_____	☆ ☆ ☆ ☆ ☆
_____	☆ ☆ ☆ ☆ ☆	_____	☆ ☆ ☆ ☆ ☆
_____	☆ ☆ ☆ ☆ ☆	_____	☆ ☆ ☆ ☆ ☆
_____	☆ ☆ ☆ ☆ ☆	_____	☆ ☆ ☆ ☆ ☆
	☆ ☆ ☆ ☆ ☆		☆ ☆ ☆ ☆ ☆

TRIP MEMORIES & OTHER NOTES:

NATIONAL PARK TRIP PLANNER:

City: _____ **State:** _____   **Anticipated Weather:**

Trip Start/End Date: _____

ACCOMMODATIONS: _____

PHONE: _____   PARK CELL RECEPTION ☐

PETS ALLOWED: ☐   PARK WIFI: ☐

SUPPLIES:

TO DO:

- ☐ LODGING RESERVATIONS
- ☐ PARK ENTRANCE PASS
- ☐ NATIONAL PARK/FED LANDS PASS
- ☐ TRIP PLAN FOR EMERGENCY CONTACT
- ☐ SAFETY LEADER: _____
- ☐ VEHICLE REGISTERED, IF REQUIRED
- ☐ DOWNLOAD NATIONAL PARK APP
- ☐ SAVED PARK FOR OFFLINE USE
- ☐ PACKED THE 10 ESSENTIALS
- ☐
- ☐
- ☐

PARK FEES

PARK ENTRANCE: _____

LODGING PER NIGHT: _____

VEHICLE REGISTRATION: _____

OTHER FEES: _____

_____

_____

ACTIVITY & PLACES TO VISIT ITINERARY

DATE/TIME	ACTIVITY	RESERVATIONS

OTHER NOTES:

NATIONAL PARK:

Overall Rating ☆ ☆ ☆ ☆ ☆

FAVORITE ACTIVITY:_____

FAVORITE TRAIL:_____

TOP WILDLIFE SIGHTS:_____

BEST SCENIC VIEWS_____

ACTIVITY ☆ ☆ ☆ ☆ ☆

LODGING ☆ ☆ ☆ ☆ ☆

FLORA & FAUNA ☆ ☆ ☆ ☆ ☆

CROWDS ☆ ☆ ☆ ☆ ☆

STARGAZING ☆ ☆ ☆ ☆ ☆

PASSPORT STAMP & MEMORABILIA

TO REMEMBER OR DO NEXT VISIT

ACTIVITY & RATING

_____	☆ ☆ ☆ ☆ ☆	_____	☆ ☆ ☆ ☆ ☆
_____	☆ ☆ ☆ ☆ ☆	_____	☆ ☆ ☆ ☆ ☆
_____	☆ ☆ ☆ ☆ ☆	_____	☆ ☆ ☆ ☆ ☆
_____	☆ ☆ ☆ ☆ ☆	_____	☆ ☆ ☆ ☆ ☆
_____	☆ ☆ ☆ ☆ ☆	_____	☆ ☆ ☆ ☆ ☆
_____	☆ ☆ ☆ ☆ ☆	_____	☆ ☆ ☆ ☆ ☆
_____	☆ ☆ ☆ ☆ ☆	_____	☆ ☆ ☆ ☆ ☆
_____	☆ ☆ ☆ ☆ ☆	_____	☆ ☆ ☆ ☆ ☆

TRIP MEMORIES & OTHER NOTES:

NATIONAL PARK TRIP PLANNER:

City: **State:**

Trip Start/End Date:_____

Anticipated Weather:

ACCOMMODATIONS: _____

PHONE: _____

PETS ALLOWED: ☐

PARK CELL RECEPTION ☐

PARK WIFI: ☐

SUPPLIES:

TO DO:

- ☐ LODGING RESERVATIONS
- ☐ PARK ENTRANCE PASS
- ☐ NATIONAL PARK/FED LANDS PASS
- ☐ TRIP PLAN FOR EMERGENCY CONTACT
- ☐ SAFETY LEADER: _____
- ☐ VEHICLE REGISTERED, IF REQUIRED
- ☐ DOWNLOAD NATIONAL PARK APP
- ☐ SAVED PARK FOR OFFLINE USE
- ☐ PACKED THE 10 ESSENTIALS
- ☐
- ☐
- ☐

PARK FEES

PARK ENTRANCE:_____

LODGING PER NIGHT:_____

VEHICLE REGISTRATION: _____

OTHER FEES:_____

_____

_____

ACTIVITY & PLACES TO VISIT ITINERARY

DATE/TIME	ACTIVITY	RESERVATIONS

OTHER NOTES:

NATIONAL PARK:

Overall Rating ☆ ☆ ☆ ☆ ☆

FAVORITE ACTIVITY:_____

FAVORITE TRAIL:_____

TOP WILDLIFE SIGHTS:_____

BEST SCENIC VIEWS_____

ACTIVITY ☆ ☆ ☆ ☆ ☆

LODGING ☆ ☆ ☆ ☆ ☆

FLORA & FAUNA ☆ ☆ ☆ ☆ ☆

CROWDS ☆ ☆ ☆ ☆ ☆

STARGAZING ☆ ☆ ☆ ☆ ☆

PASSPORT STAMP & MEMORABILIA

TO REMEMBER OR DO NEXT VISIT

ACTIVITY & RATING

_____	☆ ☆ ☆ ☆ ☆	_____	☆ ☆ ☆ ☆ ☆
_____	☆ ☆ ☆ ☆ ☆	_____	☆ ☆ ☆ ☆ ☆
_____	☆ ☆ ☆ ☆ ☆	_____	☆ ☆ ☆ ☆ ☆
_____	☆ ☆ ☆ ☆ ☆	_____	☆ ☆ ☆ ☆ ☆
_____	☆ ☆ ☆ ☆ ☆	_____	☆ ☆ ☆ ☆ ☆
_____	☆ ☆ ☆ ☆ ☆	_____	☆ ☆ ☆ ☆ ☆
_____	☆ ☆ ☆ ☆ ☆	_____	☆ ☆ ☆ ☆ ☆
	☆ ☆ ☆ ☆ ☆		☆ ☆ ☆ ☆ ☆

TRIP MEMORIES & OTHER NOTES:

NATIONAL PARK TRIP PLANNER:

City: **State:** **Anticipated Weather:**

Trip Start/End Date:_____

ACCOMMODATIONS: _____

PHONE: _____ PARK CELL RECEPTION ☐

PETS ALLOWED: ☐ PARK WIFI: ☐

SUPPLIES:

TO DO:

☐ LODGING RESERVATIONS
☐ PARK ENTRANCE PASS
☐ NATIONAL PARK/FED LANDS PASS
☐ TRIP PLAN FOR EMERGENCY
   CONTACT
☐ SAFETY LEADER: _____

PARK FEES

PARK ENTRANCE:_____

LODGING PER NIGHT:_____

VEHICLE REGISTRATION: _____

OTHER FEES:_____

_____

_____

☐ VEHICLE REGISTERED, IF
   REQUIRED
☐ DOWNLOAD NATIONAL PARK APP
☐ SAVED PARK FOR OFFLINE USE
☐ PACKED THE 10 ESSENTIALS
☐
☐
☐

ACTIVITY & PLACES TO VISIT ITINERARY

DATE/TIME	ACTIVITY	RESERVATIONS

OTHER NOTES:

NATIONAL PARK:

Overall Rating ☆ ☆ ☆ ☆ ☆

FAVORITE ACTIVITY:_____

FAVORITE TRAIL:_____

TOP WILDLIFE SIGHTS:_____

BEST SCENIC VIEWS_____

ACTIVITY ☆ ☆ ☆ ☆ ☆

LODGING ☆ ☆ ☆ ☆ ☆

FLORA & FAUNA ☆ ☆ ☆ ☆ ☆

CROWDS ☆ ☆ ☆ ☆ ☆

STARGAZING ☆ ☆ ☆ ☆ ☆

PASSPORT STAMP & MEMORABILIA

TO REMEMBER OR DO NEXT VISIT

ACTIVITY & RATING

_____	☆ ☆ ☆ ☆ ☆	_____	☆ ☆ ☆ ☆ ☆
_____	☆ ☆ ☆ ☆ ☆	_____	☆ ☆ ☆ ☆ ☆
_____	☆ ☆ ☆ ☆ ☆	_____	☆ ☆ ☆ ☆ ☆
_____	☆ ☆ ☆ ☆ ☆	_____	☆ ☆ ☆ ☆ ☆
_____	☆ ☆ ☆ ☆ ☆	_____	☆ ☆ ☆ ☆ ☆
_____	☆ ☆ ☆ ☆ ☆	_____	☆ ☆ ☆ ☆ ☆
_____	☆ ☆ ☆ ☆ ☆	_____	☆ ☆ ☆ ☆ ☆
_____	☆ ☆ ☆ ☆ ☆	_____	☆ ☆ ☆ ☆ ☆

TRIP MEMORIES & OTHER NOTES:

National Park Trip Planner:

City: _____ **State:** _____

Anticipated Weather:

Trip Start/End Date: _____

ACCOMMODATIONS: _____

PHONE: _____ PARK CELL RECEPTION ☐

PETS ALLOWED: ☐ PARK WIFI: ☐

SUPPLIES:

TO DO:

- ☐ LODGING RESERVATIONS
- ☐ PARK ENTRANCE PASS
- ☐ NATIONAL PARK/FED LANDS PASS
- ☐ TRIP PLAN FOR EMERGENCY CONTACT
- ☐ SAFETY LEADER: _____
- ☐ VEHICLE REGISTERED, IF REQUIRED
- ☐ DOWNLOAD NATIONAL PARK APP
- ☐ SAVED PARK FOR OFFLINE USE
- ☐ PACKED THE 10 ESSENTIALS
- ☐
- ☐
- ☐

PARK FEES

PARK ENTRANCE: _____

LODGING PER NIGHT: _____

VEHICLE REGISTRATION: _____

OTHER FEES: _____

_____

_____

ACTIVITY & PLACES TO VISIT ITINERARY

DATE/TIME	ACTIVITY	RESERVATIONS

OTHER NOTES:

NATIONAL PARK:

Overall Rating ☆ ☆ ☆ ☆ ☆

FAVORITE ACTIVITY:_____

FAVORITE TRAIL:_____

TOP WILDLIFE SIGHTS:_____

BEST SCENIC VIEWS_____

ACTIVITY ☆ ☆ ☆ ☆ ☆

LODGING ☆ ☆ ☆ ☆ ☆

FLORA & FAUNA ☆ ☆ ☆ ☆ ☆

CROWDS ☆ ☆ ☆ ☆ ☆

STARGAZING ☆ ☆ ☆ ☆ ☆

PASSPORT STAMP & MEMORABILIA

TO REMEMBER OR DO NEXT VISIT

ACTIVITY & RATING

_____	☆ ☆ ☆ ☆ ☆	_____	☆ ☆ ☆ ☆ ☆
_____	☆ ☆ ☆ ☆ ☆	_____	☆ ☆ ☆ ☆ ☆
_____	☆ ☆ ☆ ☆ ☆	_____	☆ ☆ ☆ ☆ ☆
_____	☆ ☆ ☆ ☆ ☆	_____	☆ ☆ ☆ ☆ ☆
_____	☆ ☆ ☆ ☆ ☆	_____	☆ ☆ ☆ ☆ ☆
_____	☆ ☆ ☆ ☆ ☆	_____	☆ ☆ ☆ ☆ ☆
_____	☆ ☆ ☆ ☆ ☆	_____	☆ ☆ ☆ ☆ ☆
	☆ ☆ ☆ ☆ ☆		☆ ☆ ☆ ☆ ☆

TRIP MEMORIES & OTHER NOTES:

NATIONAL PARK TRIP PLANNER:

City: _____ **State:** _____ **Anticipated Weather:**

Trip Start/End Date:_____

ACCOMMODATIONS: _____

PHONE: _____ PARK CELL RECEPTION ☐

PETS ALLOWED: ☐ PARK WIFI: ☐

SUPPLIES:

PARK FEES

PARK ENTRANCE:_____

LODGING PER NIGHT:_____

VEHICLE REGISTRATION: _____

OTHER FEES:_____

_____

_____

TO DO:

☐ LODGING RESERVATIONS

☐ PARK ENTRANCE PASS

☐ NATIONAL PARK/FED LANDS PASS

☐ TRIP PLAN FOR EMERGENCY CONTACT

☐ SAFETY LEADER: _____

☐ VEHICLE REGISTERED, IF REQUIRED

☐ DOWNLOAD NATIONAL PARK APP

☐ SAVED PARK FOR OFFLINE USE

☐ PACKED THE 10 ESSENTIALS

☐

☐

☐

ACTIVITY & PLACES TO VISIT ITINERARY

DATE/TIME	ACTIVITY	RESERVATIONS

OTHER NOTES:

NATIONAL PARK:

Overall Rating ☆ ☆ ☆ ☆ ☆

FAVORITE ACTIVITY:_____

FAVORITE TRAIL:_____

TOP WILDLIFE SIGHTS:_____

BEST SCENIC VIEWS_____

ACTIVITY ☆ ☆ ☆ ☆ ☆

LODGING ☆ ☆ ☆ ☆ ☆

FLORA & FAUNA ☆ ☆ ☆ ☆ ☆

CROWDS ☆ ☆ ☆ ☆ ☆

STARGAZING ☆ ☆ ☆ ☆ ☆

PASSPORT STAMP & MEMORABILIA

TO REMEMBER OR DO NEXT VISIT

ACTIVITY & RATING

_____	☆ ☆ ☆ ☆ ☆	_____	☆ ☆ ☆ ☆ ☆
_____	☆ ☆ ☆ ☆ ☆	_____	☆ ☆ ☆ ☆ ☆
_____	☆ ☆ ☆ ☆ ☆	_____	☆ ☆ ☆ ☆ ☆
_____	☆ ☆ ☆ ☆ ☆	_____	☆ ☆ ☆ ☆ ☆
_____	☆ ☆ ☆ ☆ ☆	_____	☆ ☆ ☆ ☆ ☆
_____	☆ ☆ ☆ ☆ ☆	_____	☆ ☆ ☆ ☆ ☆
_____	☆ ☆ ☆ ☆ ☆	_____	☆ ☆ ☆ ☆ ☆
	☆ ☆ ☆ ☆ ☆		☆ ☆ ☆ ☆ ☆

TRIP MEMORIES & OTHER NOTES:

NATIONAL PARK TRIP PLANNER:

City: _____ **State:** _____

Anticipated Weather:

☀ ☁ ☁ ☁ ☁ ☁ ☁ ☁

Trip Start/End Date: _____

ACCOMMODATIONS: _____

PHONE: _____ PARK CELL RECEPTION ☐

PETS ALLOWED: ☐ PARK WIFI: ☐

SUPPLIES:

TO DO:

☐ LODGING RESERVATIONS
☐ PARK ENTRANCE PASS
☐ NATIONAL PARK/FED LANDS PASS
☐ TRIP PLAN FOR EMERGENCY
   CONTACT
☐ SAFETY LEADER: _____
☐ VEHICLE REGISTERED, IF
   REQUIRED
☐ DOWNLOAD NATIONAL PARK APP
☐ SAVED PARK FOR OFFLINE USE
☐ PACKED THE 10 ESSENTIALS
☐
☐
☐

PARK FEES

PARK ENTRANCE: _____
LODGING PER NIGHT: _____
VEHICLE REGISTRATION: _____
OTHER FEES: _____
_____
_____

ACTIVITY & PLACES TO VISIT ITINERARY

DATE/TIME	ACTIVITY	RESERVATIONS

OTHER NOTES:

NATIONAL PARK:

Overall Rating ☆ ☆ ☆ ☆ ☆

FAVORITE ACTIVITY:_____

FAVORITE TRAIL:_____

TOP WILDLIFE SIGHTS:_____

BEST SCENIC VIEWS_____

ACTIVITY ☆ ☆ ☆ ☆ ☆

LODGING ☆ ☆ ☆ ☆ ☆

FLORA & FAUNA ☆ ☆ ☆ ☆ ☆

CROWDS ☆ ☆ ☆ ☆ ☆

STARGAZING ☆ ☆ ☆ ☆ ☆

PASSPORT STAMP & MEMORABILIA

TO REMEMBER OR DO NEXT VISIT

ACTIVITY & RATING

_____	☆ ☆ ☆ ☆ ☆	_____	☆ ☆ ☆ ☆ ☆
_____	☆ ☆ ☆ ☆ ☆	_____	☆ ☆ ☆ ☆ ☆
_____	☆ ☆ ☆ ☆ ☆	_____	☆ ☆ ☆ ☆ ☆
_____	☆ ☆ ☆ ☆ ☆	_____	☆ ☆ ☆ ☆ ☆
_____	☆ ☆ ☆ ☆ ☆	_____	☆ ☆ ☆ ☆ ☆
_____	☆ ☆ ☆ ☆ ☆	_____	☆ ☆ ☆ ☆ ☆
_____	☆ ☆ ☆ ☆ ☆	_____	☆ ☆ ☆ ☆ ☆
	☆ ☆ ☆ ☆ ☆		☆ ☆ ☆ ☆ ☆

TRIP MEMORIES & OTHER NOTES:

National Park Trip Planner:

City: **State:**

Trip Start/End Date: _____

Anticipated Weather:

ACCOMMODATIONS: _____

            PHONE: _____   PARK CELL RECEPTION ☐

       PETS ALLOWED: ☐   PARK WIFI: ☐

SUPPLIES:

TO DO:

- ☐ LODGING RESERVATIONS
- ☐ PARK ENTRANCE PASS
- ☐ NATIONAL PARK/FED LANDS PASS
- ☐ TRIP PLAN FOR EMERGENCY CONTACT
- ☐ SAFETY LEADER: _____
- ☐ VEHICLE REGISTERED, IF REQUIRED
- ☐ DOWNLOAD NATIONAL PARK APP
- ☐ SAVED PARK FOR OFFLINE USE
- ☐ PACKED THE 10 ESSENTIALS
- ☐
- ☐
- ☐

PARK FEES

PARK ENTRANCE: _____

LODGING PER NIGHT: _____

VEHICLE REGISTRATION: _____

OTHER FEES: _____

_____

_____

ACTIVITY & PLACES TO VISIT ITINERARY

DATE/TIME	ACTIVITY	RESERVATIONS

OTHER NOTES:

NATIONAL PARK:

Overall Rating ☆ ☆ ☆ ☆ ☆

FAVORITE ACTIVITY:_____

FAVORITE TRAIL:_____

TOP WILDLIFE SIGHTS:_____

BEST SCENIC VIEWS_____

ACTIVITY ☆ ☆ ☆ ☆ ☆

LODGING ☆ ☆ ☆ ☆ ☆

FLORA & FAUNA ☆ ☆ ☆ ☆ ☆

CROWDS ☆ ☆ ☆ ☆ ☆

STARGAZING ☆ ☆ ☆ ☆ ☆

PASSPORT STAMP & MEMORABILIA

TO REMEMBER OR DO NEXT VISIT

ACTIVITY & RATING

_____	☆ ☆ ☆ ☆ ☆	_____	☆ ☆ ☆ ☆ ☆
_____	☆ ☆ ☆ ☆ ☆	_____	☆ ☆ ☆ ☆ ☆
_____	☆ ☆ ☆ ☆ ☆	_____	☆ ☆ ☆ ☆ ☆
_____	☆ ☆ ☆ ☆ ☆	_____	☆ ☆ ☆ ☆ ☆
_____	☆ ☆ ☆ ☆ ☆	_____	☆ ☆ ☆ ☆ ☆
_____	☆ ☆ ☆ ☆ ☆	_____	☆ ☆ ☆ ☆ ☆
_____	☆ ☆ ☆ ☆ ☆	_____	☆ ☆ ☆ ☆ ☆
	☆ ☆ ☆ ☆ ☆		☆ ☆ ☆ ☆ ☆

TRIP MEMORIES & OTHER NOTES:

NATIONAL PARK TRIP PLANNER:

City: _____ **State:** _____ **Anticipated Weather:**

Trip Start/End Date:_____

ACCOMMODATIONS: _____

PHONE: _____ PARK CELL RECEPTION ☐

PETS ALLOWED: ☐ PARK WIFI: ☐

SUPPLIES:

TO DO:

☐ LODGING RESERVATIONS

☐ PARK ENTRANCE PASS

☐ NATIONAL PARK/FED LANDS PASS

☐ TRIP PLAN FOR EMERGENCY
CONTACT

☐ SAFETY LEADER: _____

☐ VEHICLE REGISTERED, IF
REQUIRED

PARK FEES

PARK ENTRANCE:_____

LODGING PER NIGHT:_____

VEHICLE REGISTRATION: _____

OTHER FEES:_____

_____

_____

☐ DOWNLOAD NATIONAL PARK APP

☐ SAVED PARK FOR OFFLINE USE

☐ PACKED THE 10 ESSENTIALS

☐

☐

☐

ACTIVITY & PLACES TO VISIT ITINERARY

DATE/TIME	ACTIVITY	RESERVATIONS

OTHER NOTES:

NATIONAL PARK:

Overall Rating ☆ ☆ ☆ ☆ ☆

FAVORITE ACTIVITY:_____

FAVORITE TRAIL:_____

TOP WILDLIFE SIGHTS:_____

BEST SCENIC VIEWS_____

ACTIVITY ☆ ☆ ☆ ☆ ☆

LODGING ☆ ☆ ☆ ☆ ☆

FLORA & FAUNA ☆ ☆ ☆ ☆ ☆

CROWDS ☆ ☆ ☆ ☆ ☆

STARGAZING ☆ ☆ ☆ ☆ ☆

PASSPORT STAMP & MEMORABILIA

TO REMEMBER OR DO NEXT VISIT

ACTIVITY & RATING

_____	☆ ☆ ☆ ☆ ☆	_____	☆ ☆ ☆ ☆ ☆
_____	☆ ☆ ☆ ☆ ☆	_____	☆ ☆ ☆ ☆ ☆
_____	☆ ☆ ☆ ☆ ☆	_____	☆ ☆ ☆ ☆ ☆
_____	☆ ☆ ☆ ☆ ☆	_____	☆ ☆ ☆ ☆ ☆
_____	☆ ☆ ☆ ☆ ☆	_____	☆ ☆ ☆ ☆ ☆
_____	☆ ☆ ☆ ☆ ☆	_____	☆ ☆ ☆ ☆ ☆
_____	☆ ☆ ☆ ☆ ☆	_____	☆ ☆ ☆ ☆ ☆
	☆ ☆ ☆ ☆ ☆		☆ ☆ ☆ ☆ ☆

TRIP MEMORIES & OTHER NOTES:

NATIONAL PARK TRIP PLANNER:

City: _____ **State:** _____

Trip Start/End Date: _____

Anticipated Weather:

☀ ⛅ ☁ 🌤 🌥 ☁ ☁ ☁

ACCOMMODATIONS: _____

PHONE: _____ PARK CELL RECEPTION ☐

PETS ALLOWED: ☐ PARK WIFI: ☐

SUPPLIES:

PARK FEES

PARK ENTRANCE: _____

LODGING PER NIGHT: _____

VEHICLE REGISTRATION: _____

OTHER FEES: _____

_____

_____

TO DO:

☐ LODGING RESERVATIONS

☐ PARK ENTRANCE PASS

☐ NATIONAL PARK/FED LANDS PASS

☐ TRIP PLAN FOR EMERGENCY CONTACT

☐ SAFETY LEADER: _____

☐ VEHICLE REGISTERED, IF REQUIRED

☐ DOWNLOAD NATIONAL PARK APP

☐ SAVED PARK FOR OFFLINE USE

☐ PACKED THE 10 ESSENTIALS

☐

☐

☐

ACTIVITY & PLACES TO VISIT ITINERARY

DATE/TIME	ACTIVITY	RESERVATIONS

OTHER NOTES:

NATIONAL PARK:

Overall Rating ☆ ☆ ☆ ☆ ☆

FAVORITE ACTIVITY:_____

FAVORITE TRAIL:_____

TOP WILDLIFE SIGHTS:_____

BEST SCENIC VIEWS_____

ACTIVITY ☆ ☆ ☆ ☆ ☆

LODGING ☆ ☆ ☆ ☆ ☆

FLORA & FAUNA ☆ ☆ ☆ ☆ ☆

CROWDS ☆ ☆ ☆ ☆ ☆

STARGAZING ☆ ☆ ☆ ☆ ☆

PASSPORT STAMP & MEMORABILIA

TO REMEMBER OR DO NEXT VISIT

ACTIVITY & RATING

_____	☆ ☆ ☆ ☆ ☆	_____	☆ ☆ ☆ ☆ ☆
_____	☆ ☆ ☆ ☆ ☆	_____	☆ ☆ ☆ ☆ ☆
_____	☆ ☆ ☆ ☆ ☆	_____	☆ ☆ ☆ ☆ ☆
_____	☆ ☆ ☆ ☆ ☆	_____	☆ ☆ ☆ ☆ ☆
_____	☆ ☆ ☆ ☆ ☆	_____	☆ ☆ ☆ ☆ ☆
_____	☆ ☆ ☆ ☆ ☆	_____	☆ ☆ ☆ ☆ ☆
_____	☆ ☆ ☆ ☆ ☆	_____	☆ ☆ ☆ ☆ ☆
_____	☆ ☆ ☆ ☆ ☆	_____	☆ ☆ ☆ ☆ ☆

TRIP MEMORIES & OTHER NOTES:

NATIONAL PARK TRIP PLANNER:

City: **State:**

Trip Start/End Date:_____

Anticipated Weather:

☼ ⛅ ☁ 🌦 🌦 ☁ ☁ 🌧

ACCOMMODATIONS: _____

PHONE: _____ PARK CELL RECEPTION ☐

PETS ALLOWED: ☐ PARK WIFI: ☐

SUPPLIES:

TO DO:

☐ LODGING RESERVATIONS
☐ PARK ENTRANCE PASS
☐ NATIONAL PARK/FED LANDS PASS
☐ TRIP PLAN FOR EMERGENCY
   CONTACT
☐ SAFETY LEADER: _____
☐ VEHICLE REGISTERED, IF
   REQUIRED
☐ DOWNLOAD NATIONAL PARK APP
☐ SAVED PARK FOR OFFLINE USE
☐ PACKED THE 10 ESSENTIALS
☐
☐
☐

PARK FEES

PARK ENTRANCE:_____

LODGING PER NIGHT:_____

VEHICLE REGISTRATION: _____

OTHER FEES:_____

_____

_____

ACTIVITY & PLACES TO VISIT ITINERARY

DATE/TIME	ACTIVITY	RESERVATIONS

OTHER NOTES:

NATIONAL PARK:

Overall Rating ☆ ☆ ☆ ☆ ☆

FAVORITE ACTIVITY:_____

FAVORITE TRAIL:_____

TOP WILDLIFE SIGHTS:_____

BEST SCENIC VIEWS_____

ACTIVITY ☆ ☆ ☆ ☆ ☆

LODGING ☆ ☆ ☆ ☆ ☆

FLORA & FAUNA ☆ ☆ ☆ ☆ ☆

CROWDS ☆ ☆ ☆ ☆ ☆

STARGAZING ☆ ☆ ☆ ☆ ☆

PASSPORT STAMP & MEMORABILIA

TO REMEMBER OR DO NEXT VISIT

ACTIVITY & RATING

_____	☆ ☆ ☆ ☆ ☆	_____	☆ ☆ ☆ ☆ ☆
_____	☆ ☆ ☆ ☆ ☆	_____	☆ ☆ ☆ ☆ ☆
_____	☆ ☆ ☆ ☆ ☆	_____	☆ ☆ ☆ ☆ ☆
_____	☆ ☆ ☆ ☆ ☆	_____	☆ ☆ ☆ ☆ ☆
_____	☆ ☆ ☆ ☆ ☆	_____	☆ ☆ ☆ ☆ ☆
_____	☆ ☆ ☆ ☆ ☆	_____	☆ ☆ ☆ ☆ ☆
_____	☆ ☆ ☆ ☆ ☆	_____	☆ ☆ ☆ ☆ ☆
	☆ ☆ ☆ ☆ ☆		☆ ☆ ☆ ☆ ☆

TRIP MEMORIES & OTHER NOTES:

NATIONAL PARK TRIP PLANNER:

City: **State:**

Trip Start/End Date:_____

Anticipated Weather:

ACCOMMODATIONS: _____

PHONE: _____   PARK CELL RECEPTION ☐

PETS ALLOWED: ☐   PARK WIFI: ☐

SUPPLIES:

TO DO:

☐ LODGING RESERVATIONS
☐ PARK ENTRANCE PASS
☐ NATIONAL PARK/FED LANDS PASS
☐ TRIP PLAN FOR EMERGENCY
   CONTACT
☐ SAFETY LEADER: _____
☐ VEHICLE REGISTERED, IF
   REQUIRED
☐ DOWNLOAD NATIONAL PARK APP
☐ SAVED PARK FOR OFFLINE USE
☐ PACKED THE 10 ESSENTIALS
☐
☐
☐

PARK FEES

PARK ENTRANCE:_____

LODGING PER NIGHT:_____

VEHICLE REGISTRATION: _____

OTHER FEES:_____

_____

_____

ACTIVITY & PLACES TO VISIT ITINERARY

DATE/TIME	ACTIVITY	RESERVATIONS

OTHER NOTES:

NATIONAL PARK:

Overall Rating ☆ ☆ ☆ ☆ ☆

FAVORITE ACTIVITY:_____

FAVORITE TRAIL:_____

TOP WILDLIFE SIGHTS:_____

BEST SCENIC VIEWS_____

ACTIVITY ☆ ☆ ☆ ☆ ☆

LODGING ☆ ☆ ☆ ☆ ☆

FLORA & FAUNA ☆ ☆ ☆ ☆ ☆

CROWDS ☆ ☆ ☆ ☆ ☆

STARGAZING ☆ ☆ ☆ ☆ ☆

PASSPORT STAMP & MEMORABILIA

TO REMEMBER OR DO NEXT VISIT

ACTIVITY & RATING

_____	☆ ☆ ☆ ☆ ☆	_____	☆ ☆ ☆ ☆ ☆
_____	☆ ☆ ☆ ☆ ☆	_____	☆ ☆ ☆ ☆ ☆
_____	☆ ☆ ☆ ☆ ☆	_____	☆ ☆ ☆ ☆ ☆
_____	☆ ☆ ☆ ☆ ☆	_____	☆ ☆ ☆ ☆ ☆
_____	☆ ☆ ☆ ☆ ☆	_____	☆ ☆ ☆ ☆ ☆
_____	☆ ☆ ☆ ☆ ☆	_____	☆ ☆ ☆ ☆ ☆
_____	☆ ☆ ☆ ☆ ☆	_____	☆ ☆ ☆ ☆ ☆
	☆ ☆ ☆ ☆ ☆		☆ ☆ ☆ ☆ ☆

TRIP MEMORIES & OTHER NOTES:

NATIONAL PARK TRIP PLANNER:

City: _____ **State:** _____

Anticipated Weather:

Trip Start/End Date: _____

ACCOMMODATIONS: _____

PHONE: _____   PARK CELL RECEPTION ☐

PETS ALLOWED: ☐   PARK WIFI: ☐

SUPPLIES:

TO DO:

☐ LODGING RESERVATIONS
☐ PARK ENTRANCE PASS
☐ NATIONAL PARK/FED LANDS PASS
☐ TRIP PLAN FOR EMERGENCY CONTACT
☐ SAFETY LEADER: _____
☐ VEHICLE REGISTERED, IF REQUIRED
☐ DOWNLOAD NATIONAL PARK APP
☐ SAVED PARK FOR OFFLINE USE
☐ PACKED THE 10 ESSENTIALS
☐
☐
☐

PARK FEES

PARK ENTRANCE: _____

LODGING PER NIGHT: _____

VEHICLE REGISTRATION: _____

OTHER FEES: _____

_____

_____

ACTIVITY & PLACES TO VISIT ITINERARY

DATE/TIME	ACTIVITY	RESERVATIONS

OTHER NOTES:

NATIONAL PARK:

Overall Rating ☆ ☆ ☆ ☆ ☆

FAVORITE ACTIVITY:_____

FAVORITE TRAIL:_____

TOP WILDLIFE SIGHTS:_____

BEST SCENIC VIEWS_____

ACTIVITY ☆ ☆ ☆ ☆ ☆

LODGING ☆ ☆ ☆ ☆ ☆

FLORA & FAUNA ☆ ☆ ☆ ☆ ☆

CROWDS ☆ ☆ ☆ ☆ ☆

STARGAZING ☆ ☆ ☆ ☆ ☆

PASSPORT STAMP & MEMORABILIA

TO REMEMBER OR DO NEXT VISIT

ACTIVITY & RATING

_____	☆ ☆ ☆ ☆ ☆	_____	☆ ☆ ☆ ☆ ☆
_____	☆ ☆ ☆ ☆ ☆	_____	☆ ☆ ☆ ☆ ☆
_____	☆ ☆ ☆ ☆ ☆	_____	☆ ☆ ☆ ☆ ☆
_____	☆ ☆ ☆ ☆ ☆	_____	☆ ☆ ☆ ☆ ☆
_____	☆ ☆ ☆ ☆ ☆	_____	☆ ☆ ☆ ☆ ☆
_____	☆ ☆ ☆ ☆ ☆	_____	☆ ☆ ☆ ☆ ☆
_____	☆ ☆ ☆ ☆ ☆	_____	☆ ☆ ☆ ☆ ☆
_____	☆ ☆ ☆ ☆ ☆	_____	☆ ☆ ☆ ☆ ☆

TRIP MEMORIES & OTHER NOTES:

NATIONAL PARK TRIP PLANNER:

City: **State:**   **Anticipated Weather:**

Trip Start/End Date: _____

ACCOMMODATIONS: _____

        PHONE: _____   PARK CELL RECEPTION ☐

    PETS ALLOWED: ☐   PARK WIFI: ☐

SUPPLIES:

TO DO:

- ☐ LODGING RESERVATIONS
- ☐ PARK ENTRANCE PASS
- ☐ NATIONAL PARK/FED LANDS PASS
- ☐ TRIP PLAN FOR EMERGENCY CONTACT
- ☐ SAFETY LEADER: _____
- ☐ VEHICLE REGISTERED, IF REQUIRED
- ☐ DOWNLOAD NATIONAL PARK APP
- ☐ SAVED PARK FOR OFFLINE USE
- ☐ PACKED THE 10 ESSENTIALS
- ☐
- ☐
- ☐

PARK FEES

PARK ENTRANCE: _____

LODGING PER NIGHT: _____

VEHICLE REGISTRATION: _____

OTHER FEES: _____

_____

_____

ACTIVITY & PLACES TO VISIT ITINERARY

DATE/TIME	ACTIVITY	RESERVATIONS

OTHER NOTES:

NATIONAL PARK:

Overall Rating ☆ ☆ ☆ ☆ ☆

FAVORITE ACTIVITY:_____

FAVORITE TRAIL:_____

TOP WILDLIFE SIGHTS:_____

BEST SCENIC VIEWS_____

ACTIVITY ☆ ☆ ☆ ☆ ☆

LODGING ☆ ☆ ☆ ☆ ☆

FLORA & FAUNA ☆ ☆ ☆ ☆ ☆

CROWDS ☆ ☆ ☆ ☆ ☆

STARGAZING ☆ ☆ ☆ ☆ ☆

PASSPORT STAMP & MEMORABILIA

TO REMEMBER OR DO NEXT VISIT

ACTIVITY & RATING

_____	☆ ☆ ☆ ☆ ☆	_____	☆ ☆ ☆ ☆ ☆
_____	☆ ☆ ☆ ☆ ☆	_____	☆ ☆ ☆ ☆ ☆
_____	☆ ☆ ☆ ☆ ☆	_____	☆ ☆ ☆ ☆ ☆
_____	☆ ☆ ☆ ☆ ☆	_____	☆ ☆ ☆ ☆ ☆
_____	☆ ☆ ☆ ☆ ☆	_____	☆ ☆ ☆ ☆ ☆
_____	☆ ☆ ☆ ☆ ☆	_____	☆ ☆ ☆ ☆ ☆
_____	☆ ☆ ☆ ☆ ☆	_____	☆ ☆ ☆ ☆ ☆
	☆ ☆ ☆ ☆ ☆		☆ ☆ ☆ ☆ ☆

TRIP MEMORIES & OTHER NOTES:

National Park Trip Planner:

City: _____ **State:** _____ **Anticipated Weather:**

Trip Start/End Date: _____

ACCOMMODATIONS: _____

PHONE: _____ PARK CELL RECEPTION ☐

PETS ALLOWED: ☐ PARK WIFI: ☐

SUPPLIES:

TO DO:

- ☐ LODGING RESERVATIONS
- ☐ PARK ENTRANCE PASS
- ☐ NATIONAL PARK/FED LANDS PASS
- ☐ TRIP PLAN FOR EMERGENCY CONTACT
- ☐ SAFETY LEADER: _____
- ☐ VEHICLE REGISTERED, IF REQUIRED
- ☐ DOWNLOAD NATIONAL PARK APP
- ☐ SAVED PARK FOR OFFLINE USE
- ☐ PACKED THE 10 ESSENTIALS
- ☐
- ☐
- ☐

PARK FEES

PARK ENTRANCE: _____

LODGING PER NIGHT: _____

VEHICLE REGISTRATION: _____

OTHER FEES: _____

_____

_____

ACTIVITY & PLACES TO VISIT ITINERARY

DATE/TIME	ACTIVITY	RESERVATIONS

OTHER NOTES:

NATIONAL PARK:

Overall Rating ☆ ☆ ☆ ☆ ☆

FAVORITE ACTIVITY:_____

FAVORITE TRAIL:_____

TOP WILDLIFE SIGHTS:_____

BEST SCENIC VIEWS_____

ACTIVITY ☆ ☆ ☆ ☆ ☆

LODGING ☆ ☆ ☆ ☆ ☆

FLORA & FAUNA ☆ ☆ ☆ ☆ ☆

CROWDS ☆ ☆ ☆ ☆ ☆

STARGAZING ☆ ☆ ☆ ☆ ☆

PASSPORT STAMP & MEMORABILIA

TO REMEMBER OR DO NEXT VISIT

ACTIVITY & RATING

_____	☆ ☆ ☆ ☆ ☆	_____	☆ ☆ ☆ ☆ ☆
_____	☆ ☆ ☆ ☆ ☆	_____	☆ ☆ ☆ ☆ ☆
_____	☆ ☆ ☆ ☆ ☆	_____	☆ ☆ ☆ ☆ ☆
_____	☆ ☆ ☆ ☆ ☆	_____	☆ ☆ ☆ ☆ ☆
_____	☆ ☆ ☆ ☆ ☆	_____	☆ ☆ ☆ ☆ ☆
_____	☆ ☆ ☆ ☆ ☆	_____	☆ ☆ ☆ ☆ ☆
_____	☆ ☆ ☆ ☆ ☆	_____	☆ ☆ ☆ ☆ ☆
_____	☆ ☆ ☆ ☆ ☆	_____	☆ ☆ ☆ ☆ ☆

TRIP MEMORIES & OTHER NOTES:

NATIONAL PARK TRIP PLANNER:

City: _____ **State:** _____

Anticipated Weather:

Trip Start/End Date: _____

ACCOMMODATIONS: _____

PHONE: _____ PARK CELL RECEPTION ☐

PETS ALLOWED: ☐ PARK WIFI: ☐

SUPPLIES:

TO DO:

☐ LODGING RESERVATIONS
☐ PARK ENTRANCE PASS
☐ NATIONAL PARK/FED LANDS PASS
☐ TRIP PLAN FOR EMERGENCY
   CONTACT
☐ SAFETY LEADER: _____
☐ VEHICLE REGISTERED, IF
   REQUIRED
☐ DOWNLOAD NATIONAL PARK APP
☐ SAVED PARK FOR OFFLINE USE
☐ PACKED THE 10 ESSENTIALS
☐
☐
☐

PARK FEES

PARK ENTRANCE: _____

LODGING PER NIGHT: _____

VEHICLE REGISTRATION: _____

OTHER FEES: _____

_____

_____

ACTIVITY & PLACES TO VISIT ITINERARY

DATE/TIME	ACTIVITY	RESERVATIONS

OTHER NOTES:

NATIONAL PARK:

Overall Rating ☆ ☆ ☆ ☆ ☆

FAVORITE ACTIVITY:_____

FAVORITE TRAIL:_____

TOP WILDLIFE SIGHTS:_____

BEST SCENIC VIEWS_____

ACTIVITY ☆ ☆ ☆ ☆ ☆

LODGING ☆ ☆ ☆ ☆ ☆

FLORA & FAUNA ☆ ☆ ☆ ☆ ☆

CROWDS ☆ ☆ ☆ ☆ ☆

STARGAZING ☆ ☆ ☆ ☆ ☆

PASSPORT STAMP & MEMORABILIA

TO REMEMBER OR DO NEXT VISIT

ACTIVITY & RATING

_____	☆ ☆ ☆ ☆ ☆	_____	☆ ☆ ☆ ☆ ☆
_____	☆ ☆ ☆ ☆ ☆	_____	☆ ☆ ☆ ☆ ☆
_____	☆ ☆ ☆ ☆ ☆	_____	☆ ☆ ☆ ☆ ☆
_____	☆ ☆ ☆ ☆ ☆	_____	☆ ☆ ☆ ☆ ☆
_____	☆ ☆ ☆ ☆ ☆	_____	☆ ☆ ☆ ☆ ☆
_____	☆ ☆ ☆ ☆ ☆	_____	☆ ☆ ☆ ☆ ☆
_____	☆ ☆ ☆ ☆ ☆	_____	☆ ☆ ☆ ☆ ☆
_____	☆ ☆ ☆ ☆ ☆	_____	☆ ☆ ☆ ☆ ☆

TRIP MEMORIES & OTHER NOTES:

NATIONAL PARK TRIP PLANNER:

City: _____ **State:** _____

Trip Start/End Date: _____

Anticipated Weather:

ACCOMMODATIONS: _____

PHONE: _____ PARK CELL RECEPTION ☐

PETS ALLOWED: ☐ PARK WIFI: ☐

SUPPLIES:

TO DO:

☐ LODGING RESERVATIONS
☐ PARK ENTRANCE PASS
☐ NATIONAL PARK/FED LANDS PASS
☐ TRIP PLAN FOR EMERGENCY
   CONTACT
☐ SAFETY LEADER: _____
☐ VEHICLE REGISTERED, IF
   REQUIRED
☐ DOWNLOAD NATIONAL PARK APP
☐ SAVED PARK FOR OFFLINE USE
☐ PACKED THE 10 ESSENTIALS
☐
☐
☐

PARK FEES

PARK ENTRANCE: _____

LODGING PER NIGHT: _____

VEHICLE REGISTRATION: _____

OTHER FEES: _____

_____

_____

ACTIVITY & PLACES TO VISIT ITINERARY

DATE/TIME	ACTIVITY	RESERVATIONS

OTHER NOTES:

NATIONAL PARK:

Overall Rating ☆ ☆ ☆ ☆ ☆

FAVORITE ACTIVITY:_____

FAVORITE TRAIL:_____

TOP WILDLIFE SIGHTS:_____

BEST SCENIC VIEWS_____

ACTIVITY ☆ ☆ ☆ ☆ ☆

LODGING ☆ ☆ ☆ ☆ ☆

FLORA & FAUNA ☆ ☆ ☆ ☆ ☆

CROWDS ☆ ☆ ☆ ☆ ☆

STARGAZING ☆ ☆ ☆ ☆ ☆

PASSPORT STAMP & MEMORABILIA

TO REMEMBER OR DO NEXT VISIT

ACTIVITY & RATING

_____	☆ ☆ ☆ ☆ ☆	_____	☆ ☆ ☆ ☆ ☆
_____	☆ ☆ ☆ ☆ ☆	_____	☆ ☆ ☆ ☆ ☆
_____	☆ ☆ ☆ ☆ ☆	_____	☆ ☆ ☆ ☆ ☆
_____	☆ ☆ ☆ ☆ ☆	_____	☆ ☆ ☆ ☆ ☆
_____	☆ ☆ ☆ ☆ ☆	_____	☆ ☆ ☆ ☆ ☆
_____	☆ ☆ ☆ ☆ ☆	_____	☆ ☆ ☆ ☆ ☆
_____	☆ ☆ ☆ ☆ ☆	_____	☆ ☆ ☆ ☆ ☆
	☆ ☆ ☆ ☆ ☆		☆ ☆ ☆ ☆ ☆

TRIP MEMORIES & OTHER NOTES:

NATIONAL PARK TRIP PLANNER:

City: **State:**

Trip Start/End Date:_____

Anticipated Weather:

ACCOMMODATIONS: _____

PHONE: _____   PARK CELL RECEPTION ☐

PETS ALLOWED: ☐   PARK WIFI: ☐

SUPPLIES:

TO DO:

☐ LODGING RESERVATIONS
☐ PARK ENTRANCE PASS
☐ NATIONAL PARK/FED LANDS PASS
☐ TRIP PLAN FOR EMERGENCY
  CONTACT
☐ SAFETY LEADER: _____
☐ VEHICLE REGISTERED, IF
  REQUIRED
☐ DOWNLOAD NATIONAL PARK APP
☐ SAVED PARK FOR OFFLINE USE
☐ PACKED THE 10 ESSENTIALS
☐
☐
☐

PARK FEES

PARK ENTRANCE:_____
LODGING PER NIGHT:_____
VEHICLE REGISTRATION: _____
OTHER FEES:_____
_____
_____

ACTIVITY & PLACES TO VISIT ITINERARY

DATE/TIME	ACTIVITY	RESERVATIONS

OTHER NOTES:

NATIONAL PARK:

Overall Rating ☆ ☆ ☆ ☆ ☆

FAVORITE ACTIVITY:_____

FAVORITE TRAIL:_____

TOP WILDLIFE SIGHTS:_____

BEST SCENIC VIEWS_____

ACTIVITY ☆ ☆ ☆ ☆ ☆

LODGING ☆ ☆ ☆ ☆ ☆

FLORA & FAUNA ☆ ☆ ☆ ☆ ☆

CROWDS ☆ ☆ ☆ ☆ ☆

STARGAZING ☆ ☆ ☆ ☆ ☆

PASSPORT STAMP & MEMORABILIA

TO REMEMBER OR DO NEXT VISIT

ACTIVITY & RATING

_____	☆ ☆ ☆ ☆ ☆	_____	☆ ☆ ☆ ☆ ☆
_____	☆ ☆ ☆ ☆ ☆	_____	☆ ☆ ☆ ☆ ☆
_____	☆ ☆ ☆ ☆ ☆	_____	☆ ☆ ☆ ☆ ☆
_____	☆ ☆ ☆ ☆ ☆	_____	☆ ☆ ☆ ☆ ☆
_____	☆ ☆ ☆ ☆ ☆	_____	☆ ☆ ☆ ☆ ☆
_____	☆ ☆ ☆ ☆ ☆	_____	☆ ☆ ☆ ☆ ☆
_____	☆ ☆ ☆ ☆ ☆	_____	☆ ☆ ☆ ☆ ☆
_____	☆ ☆ ☆ ☆ ☆	_____	☆ ☆ ☆ ☆ ☆

TRIP MEMORIES & OTHER NOTES:

NATIONAL PARK TRIP PLANNER:

City: _____ **State:** _____

Trip Start/End Date: _____

Anticipated Weather:

ACCOMMODATIONS: _____

PHONE: _____ PARK CELL RECEPTION ☐

PETS ALLOWED: ☐ PARK WIFI: ☐

SUPPLIES:

PARK FEES

PARK ENTRANCE: _____

LODGING PER NIGHT: _____

VEHICLE REGISTRATION: _____

OTHER FEES: _____

_____

_____

TO DO:

☐ LODGING RESERVATIONS

☐ PARK ENTRANCE PASS

☐ NATIONAL PARK/FED LANDS PASS

☐ TRIP PLAN FOR EMERGENCY CONTACT

☐ SAFETY LEADER: _____

☐ VEHICLE REGISTERED, IF REQUIRED

☐ DOWNLOAD NATIONAL PARK APP

☐ SAVED PARK FOR OFFLINE USE

☐ PACKED THE 10 ESSENTIALS

☐

☐

☐

ACTIVITY & PLACES TO VISIT ITINERARY

DATE/TIME	ACTIVITY	RESERVATIONS

OTHER NOTES:

NATIONAL PARK:

Overall Rating ☆ ☆ ☆ ☆ ☆

FAVORITE ACTIVITY:_____

FAVORITE TRAIL:_____

TOP WILDLIFE SIGHTS:_____

BEST SCENIC VIEWS_____

ACTIVITY ☆ ☆ ☆ ☆ ☆

LODGING ☆ ☆ ☆ ☆ ☆

FLORA & FAUNA ☆ ☆ ☆ ☆ ☆

CROWDS ☆ ☆ ☆ ☆ ☆

STARGAZING ☆ ☆ ☆ ☆ ☆

PASSPORT STAMP & MEMORABILIA

TO REMEMBER OR DO NEXT VISIT

ACTIVITY & RATING

_____	☆ ☆ ☆ ☆ ☆	_____	☆ ☆ ☆ ☆ ☆
_____	☆ ☆ ☆ ☆ ☆	_____	☆ ☆ ☆ ☆ ☆
_____	☆ ☆ ☆ ☆ ☆	_____	☆ ☆ ☆ ☆ ☆
_____	☆ ☆ ☆ ☆ ☆	_____	☆ ☆ ☆ ☆ ☆
_____	☆ ☆ ☆ ☆ ☆	_____	☆ ☆ ☆ ☆ ☆
_____	☆ ☆ ☆ ☆ ☆	_____	☆ ☆ ☆ ☆ ☆
_____	☆ ☆ ☆ ☆ ☆	_____	☆ ☆ ☆ ☆ ☆
_____	☆ ☆ ☆ ☆ ☆	_____	☆ ☆ ☆ ☆ ☆

TRIP MEMORIES & OTHER NOTES:

NATIONAL PARK TRIP PLANNER:

City: _____ **State:** _____

Trip Start/End Date: _____

Anticipated Weather:

☀ ☁ ☁ ☁ ☁ ☁ ☁ ☁

ACCOMMODATIONS: _____

PHONE: _____   PARK CELL RECEPTION ☐

PETS ALLOWED: ☐   PARK WIFI: ☐

SUPPLIES:

TO DO:
- ☐ LODGING RESERVATIONS
- ☐ PARK ENTRANCE PASS
- ☐ NATIONAL PARK/FED LANDS PASS
- ☐ TRIP PLAN FOR EMERGENCY CONTACT
- ☐ SAFETY LEADER: _____
- ☐ VEHICLE REGISTERED, IF REQUIRED
- ☐ DOWNLOAD NATIONAL PARK APP
- ☐ SAVED PARK FOR OFFLINE USE
- ☐ PACKED THE 10 ESSENTIALS
- ☐
- ☐
- ☐

PARK FEES

PARK ENTRANCE: _____

LODGING PER NIGHT: _____

VEHICLE REGISTRATION: _____

OTHER FEES: _____

_____

_____

ACTIVITY & PLACES TO VISIT ITINERARY

DATE/TIME	ACTIVITY	RESERVATIONS

OTHER NOTES:

NATIONAL PARK:

Overall Rating ☆ ☆ ☆ ☆ ☆

FAVORITE ACTIVITY: _____

FAVORITE TRAIL: _____

TOP WILDLIFE SIGHTS: _____

BEST SCENIC VIEWS _____

ACTIVITY ☆ ☆ ☆ ☆ ☆

LODGING ☆ ☆ ☆ ☆ ☆

FLORA & FAUNA ☆ ☆ ☆ ☆ ☆

CROWDS ☆ ☆ ☆ ☆ ☆

STARGAZING ☆ ☆ ☆ ☆ ☆

PASSPORT STAMP & MEMORABILIA

TO REMEMBER OR DO NEXT VISIT

ACTIVITY & RATING

_____	☆ ☆ ☆ ☆ ☆	_____	☆ ☆ ☆ ☆ ☆
_____	☆ ☆ ☆ ☆ ☆	_____	☆ ☆ ☆ ☆ ☆
_____	☆ ☆ ☆ ☆ ☆	_____	☆ ☆ ☆ ☆ ☆
_____	☆ ☆ ☆ ☆ ☆	_____	☆ ☆ ☆ ☆ ☆
_____	☆ ☆ ☆ ☆ ☆	_____	☆ ☆ ☆ ☆ ☆
_____	☆ ☆ ☆ ☆ ☆	_____	☆ ☆ ☆ ☆ ☆
_____	☆ ☆ ☆ ☆ ☆	_____	☆ ☆ ☆ ☆ ☆
_____	☆ ☆ ☆ ☆ ☆	_____	☆ ☆ ☆ ☆ ☆

TRIP MEMORIES & OTHER NOTES:

NATIONAL PARK TRIP PLANNER:

City: **State:**

Trip Start/End Date:_____

Anticipated Weather:

ACCOMMODATIONS: _____

PHONE: _____ PARK CELL RECEPTION ☐

PETS ALLOWED: ☐ PARK WIFI: ☐

SUPPLIES:

TO DO:

☐ LODGING RESERVATIONS
☐ PARK ENTRANCE PASS
☐ NATIONAL PARK/FED LANDS PASS
☐ TRIP PLAN FOR EMERGENCY
  CONTACT
☐ SAFETY LEADER: _____
☐ VEHICLE REGISTERED, IF
  REQUIRED
☐ DOWNLOAD NATIONAL PARK APP
☐ SAVED PARK FOR OFFLINE USE
☐ PACKED THE 10 ESSENTIALS
☐
☐
☐

PARK FEES

PARK ENTRANCE:_____

LODGING PER NIGHT:_____

VEHICLE REGISTRATION: _____

OTHER FEES:_____

_____

_____

ACTIVITY & PLACES TO VISIT ITINERARY

DATE/TIME	ACTIVITY	RESERVATIONS

OTHER NOTES:

NATIONAL PARK:

Overall Rating ☆ ☆ ☆ ☆ ☆

FAVORITE ACTIVITY:_____

FAVORITE TRAIL:_____

TOP WILDLIFE SIGHTS:_____

BEST SCENIC VIEWS_____

ACTIVITY ☆ ☆ ☆ ☆ ☆

LODGING ☆ ☆ ☆ ☆ ☆

FLORA & FAUNA ☆ ☆ ☆ ☆ ☆

CROWDS ☆ ☆ ☆ ☆ ☆

STARGAZING ☆ ☆ ☆ ☆ ☆

PASSPORT STAMP & MEMORABILIA

TO REMEMBER OR DO NEXT VISIT

ACTIVITY & RATING

_____	☆ ☆ ☆ ☆ ☆	_____	☆ ☆ ☆ ☆ ☆
_____	☆ ☆ ☆ ☆ ☆	_____	☆ ☆ ☆ ☆ ☆
_____	☆ ☆ ☆ ☆ ☆	_____	☆ ☆ ☆ ☆ ☆
_____	☆ ☆ ☆ ☆ ☆	_____	☆ ☆ ☆ ☆ ☆
_____	☆ ☆ ☆ ☆ ☆	_____	☆ ☆ ☆ ☆ ☆
_____	☆ ☆ ☆ ☆ ☆	_____	☆ ☆ ☆ ☆ ☆
_____	☆ ☆ ☆ ☆ ☆	_____	☆ ☆ ☆ ☆ ☆
_____	☆ ☆ ☆ ☆ ☆	_____	☆ ☆ ☆ ☆ ☆

TRIP MEMORIES & OTHER NOTES:

NATIONAL PARK TRIP PLANNER:

City: **State:**

Anticipated Weather:

Trip Start/End Date: _____

ACCOMMODATIONS: _____

PHONE: _____

PARK CELL RECEPTION ☐

PETS ALLOWED: ☐

PARK WIFI: ☐

SUPPLIES:

TO DO:

- ☐ LODGING RESERVATIONS
- ☐ PARK ENTRANCE PASS
- ☐ NATIONAL PARK/FED LANDS PASS
- ☐ TRIP PLAN FOR EMERGENCY CONTACT
- ☐ SAFETY LEADER: _____
- ☐ VEHICLE REGISTERED, IF REQUIRED
- ☐ DOWNLOAD NATIONAL PARK APP
- ☐ SAVED PARK FOR OFFLINE USE
- ☐ PACKED THE 10 ESSENTIALS
- ☐
- ☐
- ☐

PARK FEES

PARK ENTRANCE: _____

LODGING PER NIGHT: _____

VEHICLE REGISTRATION: _____

OTHER FEES: _____

_____

_____

ACTIVITY & PLACES TO VISIT ITINERARY

DATE/TIME	ACTIVITY	RESERVATIONS

OTHER NOTES:

NATIONAL PARK:

Overall Rating ☆ ☆ ☆ ☆ ☆

FAVORITE ACTIVITY:_____

FAVORITE TRAIL:_____

TOP WILDLIFE SIGHTS:_____

BEST SCENIC VIEWS_____

ACTIVITY ☆ ☆ ☆ ☆ ☆

LODGING ☆ ☆ ☆ ☆ ☆

FLORA & FAUNA ☆ ☆ ☆ ☆ ☆

CROWDS ☆ ☆ ☆ ☆ ☆

STARGAZING ☆ ☆ ☆ ☆ ☆

PASSPORT STAMP & MEMORABILIA

TO REMEMBER OR DO NEXT VISIT

ACTIVITY & RATING

_____	☆ ☆ ☆ ☆ ☆	_____	☆ ☆ ☆ ☆ ☆
_____	☆ ☆ ☆ ☆ ☆	_____	☆ ☆ ☆ ☆ ☆
_____	☆ ☆ ☆ ☆ ☆	_____	☆ ☆ ☆ ☆ ☆
_____	☆ ☆ ☆ ☆ ☆	_____	☆ ☆ ☆ ☆ ☆
_____	☆ ☆ ☆ ☆ ☆	_____	☆ ☆ ☆ ☆ ☆
_____	☆ ☆ ☆ ☆ ☆	_____	☆ ☆ ☆ ☆ ☆
_____	☆ ☆ ☆ ☆ ☆	_____	☆ ☆ ☆ ☆ ☆
_____	☆ ☆ ☆ ☆ ☆	_____	☆ ☆ ☆ ☆ ☆

TRIP MEMORIES & OTHER NOTES:

NATIONAL PARK TRIP PLANNER:

City: _____ State: _____

Trip Start/End Date: _____

Anticipated Weather:

ACCOMMODATIONS: _____

PHONE: _____ PARK CELL RECEPTION ☐

PETS ALLOWED: ☐ PARK WIFI: ☐

SUPPLIES:

TO DO:

- ☐ LODGING RESERVATIONS
- ☐ PARK ENTRANCE PASS
- ☐ NATIONAL PARK/FED LANDS PASS
- ☐ TRIP PLAN FOR EMERGENCY CONTACT
- ☐ SAFETY LEADER: _____
- ☐ VEHICLE REGISTERED, IF REQUIRED
- ☐ DOWNLOAD NATIONAL PARK APP
- ☐ SAVED PARK FOR OFFLINE USE
- ☐ PACKED THE 10 ESSENTIALS
- ☐
- ☐
- ☐

PARK FEES

PARK ENTRANCE: _____

LODGING PER NIGHT: _____

VEHICLE REGISTRATION: _____

OTHER FEES: _____

_____

_____

ACTIVITY & PLACES TO VISIT ITINERARY

DATE/TIME	ACTIVITY	RESERVATIONS

OTHER NOTES:

NATIONAL PARK:

Overall Rating ☆ ☆ ☆ ☆ ☆

FAVORITE ACTIVITY:_____

FAVORITE TRAIL:_____

TOP WILDLIFE SIGHTS:_____

BEST SCENIC VIEWS_____

ACTIVITY ☆ ☆ ☆ ☆ ☆

LODGING ☆ ☆ ☆ ☆ ☆

FLORA & FAUNA ☆ ☆ ☆ ☆ ☆

CROWDS ☆ ☆ ☆ ☆ ☆

STARGAZING ☆ ☆ ☆ ☆ ☆

PASSPORT STAMP & MEMORABILIA

TO REMEMBER OR DO NEXT VISIT

ACTIVITY & RATING

_____	☆ ☆ ☆ ☆ ☆	_____	☆ ☆ ☆ ☆ ☆
_____	☆ ☆ ☆ ☆ ☆	_____	☆ ☆ ☆ ☆ ☆
_____	☆ ☆ ☆ ☆ ☆	_____	☆ ☆ ☆ ☆ ☆
_____	☆ ☆ ☆ ☆ ☆	_____	☆ ☆ ☆ ☆ ☆
_____	☆ ☆ ☆ ☆ ☆	_____	☆ ☆ ☆ ☆ ☆
_____	☆ ☆ ☆ ☆ ☆	_____	☆ ☆ ☆ ☆ ☆
_____	☆ ☆ ☆ ☆ ☆	_____	☆ ☆ ☆ ☆ ☆
_____	☆ ☆ ☆ ☆ ☆	_____	☆ ☆ ☆ ☆ ☆

TRIP MEMORIES & OTHER NOTES:

NATIONAL PARK TRIP PLANNER:

City: _____ **State:** _____

Anticipated Weather:

Trip Start/End Date:_____

ACCOMMODATIONS: _____

PHONE: _____   PARK CELL RECEPTION ☐

PETS ALLOWED: ☐   PARK WIFI: ☐

SUPPLIES:

TO DO:

- ☐ LODGING RESERVATIONS
- ☐ PARK ENTRANCE PASS
- ☐ NATIONAL PARK/FED LANDS PASS
- ☐ TRIP PLAN FOR EMERGENCY CONTACT
- ☐ SAFETY LEADER: _____
- ☐ VEHICLE REGISTERED, IF REQUIRED
- ☐ DOWNLOAD NATIONAL PARK APP
- ☐ SAVED PARK FOR OFFLINE USE
- ☐ PACKED THE 10 ESSENTIALS
- ☐
- ☐
- ☐

PARK FEES

PARK ENTRANCE:_____

LODGING PER NIGHT:_____

VEHICLE REGISTRATION: _____

OTHER FEES:_____

_____

_____

ACTIVITY & PLACES TO VISIT ITINERARY

DATE/TIME	ACTIVITY	RESERVATIONS

OTHER NOTES:

NATIONAL PARK:

Overall Rating ☆ ☆ ☆ ☆ ☆

FAVORITE ACTIVITY:_____

FAVORITE TRAIL:_____

TOP WILDLIFE SIGHTS:_____

BEST SCENIC VIEWS_____

ACTIVITY ☆ ☆ ☆ ☆ ☆

LODGING ☆ ☆ ☆ ☆ ☆

FLORA & FAUNA ☆ ☆ ☆ ☆ ☆

CROWDS ☆ ☆ ☆ ☆ ☆

STARGAZING ☆ ☆ ☆ ☆ ☆

PASSPORT STAMP & MEMORABILIA

TO REMEMBER OR DO NEXT VISIT

ACTIVITY & RATING

_____	☆ ☆ ☆ ☆ ☆	_____ ☆ ☆ ☆ ☆ ☆
_____	☆ ☆ ☆ ☆ ☆	_____ ☆ ☆ ☆ ☆ ☆
_____	☆ ☆ ☆ ☆ ☆	_____ ☆ ☆ ☆ ☆ ☆
_____	☆ ☆ ☆ ☆ ☆	_____ ☆ ☆ ☆ ☆ ☆
_____	☆ ☆ ☆ ☆ ☆	_____ ☆ ☆ ☆ ☆ ☆
_____	☆ ☆ ☆ ☆ ☆	_____ ☆ ☆ ☆ ☆ ☆
_____	☆ ☆ ☆ ☆ ☆	_____ ☆ ☆ ☆ ☆ ☆
_____	☆ ☆ ☆ ☆ ☆	_____ ☆ ☆ ☆ ☆ ☆

TRIP MEMORIES & OTHER NOTES:

NATIONAL PARK TRIP PLANNER:

City: _____ **State:** _____

Trip Start/End Date: _____

Anticipated Weather:

ACCOMMODATIONS: _____

PHONE: _____

PETS ALLOWED: ☐

PARK CELL RECEPTION ☐

PARK WIFI: ☐

SUPPLIES:

PARK FEES

PARK ENTRANCE: _____

LODGING PER NIGHT: _____

VEHICLE REGISTRATION: _____

OTHER FEES: _____

_____

_____

TO DO:

☐ LODGING RESERVATIONS

☐ PARK ENTRANCE PASS

☐ NATIONAL PARK/FED LANDS PASS

☐ TRIP PLAN FOR EMERGENCY
CONTACT

☐ SAFETY LEADER: _____

☐ VEHICLE REGISTERED, IF
REQUIRED

☐ DOWNLOAD NATIONAL PARK APP

☐ SAVED PARK FOR OFFLINE USE

☐ PACKED THE 10 ESSENTIALS

☐

☐

☐

ACTIVITY & PLACES TO VISIT ITINERARY

DATE/TIME	ACTIVITY	RESERVATIONS

OTHER NOTES:

NATIONAL PARK:

Overall Rating ☆ ☆ ☆ ☆ ☆

FAVORITE ACTIVITY:_____

FAVORITE TRAIL:_____

TOP WILDLIFE SIGHTS:_____

BEST SCENIC VIEWS_____

ACTIVITY ☆ ☆ ☆ ☆ ☆

LODGING ☆ ☆ ☆ ☆ ☆

FLORA & FAUNA ☆ ☆ ☆ ☆ ☆

CROWDS ☆ ☆ ☆ ☆ ☆

STARGAZING ☆ ☆ ☆ ☆ ☆

PASSPORT STAMP & MEMORABILIA

TO REMEMBER OR DO NEXT VISIT

ACTIVITY & RATING

_____	☆ ☆ ☆ ☆ ☆	_____	☆ ☆ ☆ ☆ ☆
_____	☆ ☆ ☆ ☆ ☆	_____	☆ ☆ ☆ ☆ ☆
_____	☆ ☆ ☆ ☆ ☆	_____	☆ ☆ ☆ ☆ ☆
_____	☆ ☆ ☆ ☆ ☆	_____	☆ ☆ ☆ ☆ ☆
_____	☆ ☆ ☆ ☆ ☆	_____	☆ ☆ ☆ ☆ ☆
_____	☆ ☆ ☆ ☆ ☆	_____	☆ ☆ ☆ ☆ ☆
_____	☆ ☆ ☆ ☆ ☆	_____	☆ ☆ ☆ ☆ ☆
_____	☆ ☆ ☆ ☆ ☆	_____	☆ ☆ ☆ ☆ ☆

TRIP MEMORIES & OTHER NOTES:

NATIONAL PARK TRIP PLANNER:

City: _____ **State:** _____

Anticipated Weather:

Trip Start/End Date: _____

ACCOMMODATIONS: _____

                   PHONE: _____   PARK CELL RECEPTION ☐

        PETS ALLOWED: ☐   PARK WIFI: ☐

SUPPLIES:

TO DO:

- ☐ LODGING RESERVATIONS
- ☐ PARK ENTRANCE PASS
- ☐ NATIONAL PARK/FED LANDS PASS
- ☐ TRIP PLAN FOR EMERGENCY CONTACT
- ☐ SAFETY LEADER: _____
- ☐ VEHICLE REGISTERED, IF REQUIRED
- ☐ DOWNLOAD NATIONAL PARK APP
- ☐ SAVED PARK FOR OFFLINE USE
- ☐ PACKED THE 10 ESSENTIALS
- ☐
- ☐
- ☐

PARK FEES

PARK ENTRANCE: _____

LODGING PER NIGHT: _____

VEHICLE REGISTRATION: _____

OTHER FEES: _____

_____

_____

ACTIVITY & PLACES TO VISIT ITINERARY

DATE/TIME	ACTIVITY	RESERVATIONS

OTHER NOTES:

NATIONAL PARK:

Overall Rating ☆ ☆ ☆ ☆ ☆

FAVORITE ACTIVITY: _____

FAVORITE TRAIL: _____

TOP WILDLIFE SIGHTS: _____

BEST SCENIC VIEWS _____

ACTIVITY ☆ ☆ ☆ ☆ ☆

LODGING ☆ ☆ ☆ ☆ ☆

FLORA & FAUNA ☆ ☆ ☆ ☆ ☆

CROWDS ☆ ☆ ☆ ☆ ☆

STARGAZING ☆ ☆ ☆ ☆ ☆

PASSPORT STAMP & MEMORABILIA

TO REMEMBER OR DO NEXT VISIT

ACTIVITY & RATING

_____	☆ ☆ ☆ ☆ ☆	_____	☆ ☆ ☆ ☆ ☆
_____	☆ ☆ ☆ ☆ ☆	_____	☆ ☆ ☆ ☆ ☆
_____	☆ ☆ ☆ ☆ ☆	_____	☆ ☆ ☆ ☆ ☆
_____	☆ ☆ ☆ ☆ ☆	_____	☆ ☆ ☆ ☆ ☆
_____	☆ ☆ ☆ ☆ ☆	_____	☆ ☆ ☆ ☆ ☆
_____	☆ ☆ ☆ ☆ ☆	_____	☆ ☆ ☆ ☆ ☆
_____	☆ ☆ ☆ ☆ ☆	_____	☆ ☆ ☆ ☆ ☆
	☆ ☆ ☆ ☆ ☆		☆ ☆ ☆ ☆ ☆

TRIP MEMORIES & OTHER NOTES:

NATIONAL PARK TRIP PLANNER:

City: _____ **State:** _____

Trip Start/End Date: _____

Anticipated Weather:

ACCOMMODATIONS: _____

PHONE: _____   PARK CELL RECEPTION ☐

PETS ALLOWED: ☐   PARK WIFI: ☐

SUPPLIES:

PARK FEES

PARK ENTRANCE: _____

LODGING PER NIGHT: _____

VEHICLE REGISTRATION: _____

OTHER FEES: _____

_____

_____

TO DO:

☐ LODGING RESERVATIONS

☐ PARK ENTRANCE PASS

☐ NATIONAL PARK/FED LANDS PASS

☐ TRIP PLAN FOR EMERGENCY CONTACT

☐ SAFETY LEADER: _____

☐ VEHICLE REGISTERED, IF REQUIRED

☐ DOWNLOAD NATIONAL PARK APP

☐ SAVED PARK FOR OFFLINE USE

☐ PACKED THE 10 ESSENTIALS

☐

☐

☐

ACTIVITY & PLACES TO VISIT ITINERARY

DATE/TIME	ACTIVITY	RESERVATIONS

OTHER NOTES:

NATIONAL PARK:

Overall Rating ☆ ☆ ☆ ☆ ☆

FAVORITE ACTIVITY:_____

FAVORITE TRAIL:_____

TOP WILDLIFE SIGHTS:_____

BEST SCENIC VIEWS_____

ACTIVITY ☆ ☆ ☆ ☆ ☆

LODGING ☆ ☆ ☆ ☆ ☆

FLORA & FAUNA ☆ ☆ ☆ ☆ ☆

CROWDS ☆ ☆ ☆ ☆ ☆

STARGAZING ☆ ☆ ☆ ☆ ☆

TO REMEMBER OR DO NEXT VISIT

PASSPORT STAMP & MEMORABILIA

ACTIVITY & RATING

_____	☆ ☆ ☆ ☆ ☆	_____	☆ ☆ ☆ ☆ ☆
_____	☆ ☆ ☆ ☆ ☆	_____	☆ ☆ ☆ ☆ ☆
_____	☆ ☆ ☆ ☆ ☆	_____	☆ ☆ ☆ ☆ ☆
_____	☆ ☆ ☆ ☆ ☆	_____	☆ ☆ ☆ ☆ ☆
_____	☆ ☆ ☆ ☆ ☆	_____	☆ ☆ ☆ ☆ ☆
_____	☆ ☆ ☆ ☆ ☆	_____	☆ ☆ ☆ ☆ ☆
_____	☆ ☆ ☆ ☆ ☆	_____	☆ ☆ ☆ ☆ ☆
	☆ ☆ ☆ ☆ ☆		☆ ☆ ☆ ☆ ☆

TRIP MEMORIES & OTHER NOTES:

NATIONAL PARK TRIP PLANNER:

City: _____ State: _____

Trip Start/End Date: _____

Anticipated Weather:

ACCOMMODATIONS: _____

PHONE: _____   PARK CELL RECEPTION ☐

PETS ALLOWED: ☐   PARK WIFI: ☐

SUPPLIES:

TO DO:

- ☐ LODGING RESERVATIONS
- ☐ PARK ENTRANCE PASS
- ☐ NATIONAL PARK/FED LANDS PASS
- ☐ TRIP PLAN FOR EMERGENCY CONTACT
- ☐ SAFETY LEADER: _____
- ☐ VEHICLE REGISTERED, IF REQUIRED
- ☐ DOWNLOAD NATIONAL PARK APP
- ☐ SAVED PARK FOR OFFLINE USE
- ☐ PACKED THE 10 ESSENTIALS
- ☐
- ☐
- ☐

PARK FEES

PARK ENTRANCE: _____

LODGING PER NIGHT: _____

VEHICLE REGISTRATION: _____

OTHER FEES: _____

_____

_____

ACTIVITY & PLACES TO VISIT ITINERARY

DATE/TIME	ACTIVITY	RESERVATIONS

OTHER NOTES:

NATIONAL PARK:

Overall Rating ☆ ☆ ☆ ☆ ☆

FAVORITE ACTIVITY: _____

FAVORITE TRAIL: _____

TOP WILDLIFE SIGHTS: _____

BEST SCENIC VIEWS _____

ACTIVITY ☆ ☆ ☆ ☆ ☆

LODGING ☆ ☆ ☆ ☆ ☆

FLORA & FAUNA ☆ ☆ ☆ ☆ ☆

CROWDS ☆ ☆ ☆ ☆ ☆

STARGAZING ☆ ☆ ☆ ☆ ☆

PASSPORT STAMP & MEMORABILIA

TO REMEMBER OR DO NEXT VISIT

ACTIVITY & RATING

_____	☆ ☆ ☆ ☆ ☆	_____	☆ ☆ ☆ ☆ ☆
_____	☆ ☆ ☆ ☆ ☆	_____	☆ ☆ ☆ ☆ ☆
_____	☆ ☆ ☆ ☆ ☆	_____	☆ ☆ ☆ ☆ ☆
_____	☆ ☆ ☆ ☆ ☆	_____	☆ ☆ ☆ ☆ ☆
_____	☆ ☆ ☆ ☆ ☆	_____	☆ ☆ ☆ ☆ ☆
_____	☆ ☆ ☆ ☆ ☆	_____	☆ ☆ ☆ ☆ ☆
_____	☆ ☆ ☆ ☆ ☆	_____	☆ ☆ ☆ ☆ ☆
	☆ ☆ ☆ ☆ ☆		☆ ☆ ☆ ☆ ☆

TRIP MEMORIES & OTHER NOTES:

NATIONAL PARK TRIP PLANNER:

City: **State:**   **Anticipated Weather:**

Trip Start/End Date: _____

ACCOMMODATIONS: _____

            PHONE: _____   PARK CELL RECEPTION ☐

      PETS ALLOWED: ☐   PARK WIFI: ☐

SUPPLIES:

TO DO:

- ☐ LODGING RESERVATIONS
- ☐ PARK ENTRANCE PASS
- ☐ NATIONAL PARK/FED LANDS PASS
- ☐ TRIP PLAN FOR EMERGENCY CONTACT
- ☐ SAFETY LEADER: _____
- ☐ VEHICLE REGISTERED, IF REQUIRED
- ☐ DOWNLOAD NATIONAL PARK APP
- ☐ SAVED PARK FOR OFFLINE USE
- ☐ PACKED THE 10 ESSENTIALS
- ☐
- ☐
- ☐

PARK FEES

PARK ENTRANCE: _____

LODGING PER NIGHT: _____

VEHICLE REGISTRATION: _____

OTHER FEES: _____

_____

_____

ACTIVITY & PLACES TO VISIT ITINERARY

DATE/TIME	ACTIVITY	RESERVATIONS

OTHER NOTES:

NATIONAL PARK:

Overall Rating ☆ ☆ ☆ ☆ ☆

FAVORITE ACTIVITY: _____

FAVORITE TRAIL: _____

TOP WILDLIFE SIGHTS: _____

BEST SCENIC VIEWS _____

ACTIVITY ☆ ☆ ☆ ☆ ☆

LODGING ☆ ☆ ☆ ☆ ☆

FLORA & FAUNA ☆ ☆ ☆ ☆ ☆

CROWDS ☆ ☆ ☆ ☆ ☆

STARGAZING ☆ ☆ ☆ ☆ ☆

PASSPORT STAMP & MEMORABILIA

TO REMEMBER OR DO NEXT VISIT

ACTIVITY & RATING

_____	☆ ☆ ☆ ☆ ☆	_____	☆ ☆ ☆ ☆ ☆
_____	☆ ☆ ☆ ☆ ☆	_____	☆ ☆ ☆ ☆ ☆
_____	☆ ☆ ☆ ☆ ☆	_____	☆ ☆ ☆ ☆ ☆
_____	☆ ☆ ☆ ☆ ☆	_____	☆ ☆ ☆ ☆ ☆
_____	☆ ☆ ☆ ☆ ☆	_____	☆ ☆ ☆ ☆ ☆
_____	☆ ☆ ☆ ☆ ☆	_____	☆ ☆ ☆ ☆ ☆
_____	☆ ☆ ☆ ☆ ☆	_____	☆ ☆ ☆ ☆ ☆
	☆ ☆ ☆ ☆ ☆		☆ ☆ ☆ ☆ ☆

TRIP MEMORIES & OTHER NOTES:

NATIONAL PARK TRIP PLANNER:

City: _____ **State:** _____

Anticipated Weather:

Trip Start/End Date:_____

ACCOMMODATIONS: _____

PHONE: _____ PARK CELL RECEPTION ☐

PETS ALLOWED: ☐ PARK WIFI: ☐

SUPPLIES:

PARK FEES

PARK ENTRANCE:_____

LODGING PER NIGHT:_____

VEHICLE REGISTRATION: _____

OTHER FEES:_____

_____

_____

TO DO:

☐ LODGING RESERVATIONS

☐ PARK ENTRANCE PASS

☐ NATIONAL PARK/FED LANDS PASS

☐ TRIP PLAN FOR EMERGENCY CONTACT

☐ SAFETY LEADER: _____

☐ VEHICLE REGISTERED, IF REQUIRED

☐ DOWNLOAD NATIONAL PARK APP

☐ SAVED PARK FOR OFFLINE USE

☐ PACKED THE 10 ESSENTIALS

☐

☐

☐

ACTIVITY & PLACES TO VISIT ITINERARY

DATE/TIME	ACTIVITY	RESERVATIONS

OTHER NOTES:

NATIONAL PARK:

Overall Rating ☆ ☆ ☆ ☆ ☆

FAVORITE ACTIVITY:_____

FAVORITE TRAIL:_____

TOP WILDLIFE SIGHTS:_____

BEST SCENIC VIEWS_____

ACTIVITY ☆ ☆ ☆ ☆ ☆

LODGING ☆ ☆ ☆ ☆ ☆

FLORA & FAUNA ☆ ☆ ☆ ☆ ☆

CROWDS ☆ ☆ ☆ ☆ ☆

STARGAZING ☆ ☆ ☆ ☆ ☆

PASSPORT STAMP & MEMORABILIA

TO REMEMBER OR DO NEXT VISIT

ACTIVITY & RATING

_____	☆ ☆ ☆ ☆ ☆	_____	☆ ☆ ☆ ☆ ☆
_____	☆ ☆ ☆ ☆ ☆	_____	☆ ☆ ☆ ☆ ☆
_____	☆ ☆ ☆ ☆ ☆	_____	☆ ☆ ☆ ☆ ☆
_____	☆ ☆ ☆ ☆ ☆	_____	☆ ☆ ☆ ☆ ☆
_____	☆ ☆ ☆ ☆ ☆	_____	☆ ☆ ☆ ☆ ☆
_____	☆ ☆ ☆ ☆ ☆	_____	☆ ☆ ☆ ☆ ☆
_____	☆ ☆ ☆ ☆ ☆	_____	☆ ☆ ☆ ☆ ☆
	☆ ☆ ☆ ☆ ☆		☆ ☆ ☆ ☆ ☆

TRIP MEMORIES & OTHER NOTES:

NATIONAL PARK TRIP PLANNER:

City: **State:**

Trip Start/End Date:_____

Anticipated Weather:

ACCOMMODATIONS: _____

PHONE: _____ PARK CELL RECEPTION ☐

PETS ALLOWED: ☐ PARK WIFI: ☐

SUPPLIES:

PARK FEES

PARK ENTRANCE:_____

LODGING PER NIGHT:_____

VEHICLE REGISTRATION: _____

OTHER FEES:_____

_____

_____

TO DO:

☐ LODGING RESERVATIONS

☐ PARK ENTRANCE PASS

☐ NATIONAL PARK/FED LANDS PASS

☐ TRIP PLAN FOR EMERGENCY CONTACT

☐ SAFETY LEADER: _____

☐ VEHICLE REGISTERED, IF REQUIRED

☐ DOWNLOAD NATIONAL PARK APP

☐ SAVED PARK FOR OFFLINE USE

☐ PACKED THE 10 ESSENTIALS

☐

☐

☐

ACTIVITY & PLACES TO VISIT ITINERARY

DATE/TIME	ACTIVITY	RESERVATIONS

OTHER NOTES:

NATIONAL PARK:

Overall Rating ☆ ☆ ☆ ☆ ☆

FAVORITE ACTIVITY:_____

FAVORITE TRAIL:_____

TOP WILDLIFE SIGHTS:_____

BEST SCENIC VIEWS_____

ACTIVITY ☆ ☆ ☆ ☆ ☆

LODGING ☆ ☆ ☆ ☆ ☆

FLORA & FAUNA ☆ ☆ ☆ ☆ ☆

CROWDS ☆ ☆ ☆ ☆ ☆

STARGAZING ☆ ☆ ☆ ☆ ☆

PASSPORT STAMP & MEMORABILIA

TO REMEMBER OR DO NEXT VISIT

ACTIVITY & RATING

_____	☆ ☆ ☆ ☆ ☆	_____	☆ ☆ ☆ ☆ ☆
_____	☆ ☆ ☆ ☆ ☆	_____	☆ ☆ ☆ ☆ ☆
_____	☆ ☆ ☆ ☆ ☆	_____	☆ ☆ ☆ ☆ ☆
_____	☆ ☆ ☆ ☆ ☆	_____	☆ ☆ ☆ ☆ ☆
_____	☆ ☆ ☆ ☆ ☆	_____	☆ ☆ ☆ ☆ ☆
_____	☆ ☆ ☆ ☆ ☆	_____	☆ ☆ ☆ ☆ ☆
_____	☆ ☆ ☆ ☆ ☆	_____	☆ ☆ ☆ ☆ ☆
_____	☆ ☆ ☆ ☆ ☆	_____	☆ ☆ ☆ ☆ ☆

TRIP MEMORIES & OTHER NOTES:

NATIONAL PARK TRIP PLANNER:

City: _____ **State:** _____

Trip Start/End Date:_____

Anticipated Weather:

ACCOMMODATIONS: _____

PHONE: _____ PARK CELL RECEPTION ☐

PETS ALLOWED: ☐ PARK WIFI: ☐

SUPPLIES:

TO DO:

☐ LODGING RESERVATIONS

☐ PARK ENTRANCE PASS

☐ NATIONAL PARK/FED LANDS PASS

☐ TRIP PLAN FOR EMERGENCY CONTACT

☐ SAFETY LEADER: _____

☐ VEHICLE REGISTERED, IF REQUIRED

☐ DOWNLOAD NATIONAL PARK APP

☐ SAVED PARK FOR OFFLINE USE

☐ PACKED THE 10 ESSENTIALS

☐

☐

☐

PARK FEES

PARK ENTRANCE:_____

LODGING PER NIGHT:_____

VEHICLE REGISTRATION: _____

OTHER FEES:_____

_____

_____

ACTIVITY & PLACES TO VISIT ITINERARY

DATE/TIME	ACTIVITY	RESERVATIONS

OTHER NOTES:

NATIONAL PARK:

Overall Rating ☆ ☆ ☆ ☆ ☆

FAVORITE ACTIVITY:_____

FAVORITE TRAIL:_____

TOP WILDLIFE SIGHTS:_____

BEST SCENIC VIEWS_____

ACTIVITY ☆ ☆ ☆ ☆ ☆

LODGING ☆ ☆ ☆ ☆ ☆

FLORA & FAUNA ☆ ☆ ☆ ☆ ☆

CROWDS ☆ ☆ ☆ ☆ ☆

STARGAZING ☆ ☆ ☆ ☆ ☆

PASSPORT STAMP & MEMORABILIA

TO REMEMBER OR DO NEXT VISIT

ACTIVITY & RATING

_____	☆ ☆ ☆ ☆ ☆	_____	☆ ☆ ☆ ☆ ☆
_____	☆ ☆ ☆ ☆ ☆	_____	☆ ☆ ☆ ☆ ☆
_____	☆ ☆ ☆ ☆ ☆	_____	☆ ☆ ☆ ☆ ☆
_____	☆ ☆ ☆ ☆ ☆	_____	☆ ☆ ☆ ☆ ☆
_____	☆ ☆ ☆ ☆ ☆	_____	☆ ☆ ☆ ☆ ☆
_____	☆ ☆ ☆ ☆ ☆	_____	☆ ☆ ☆ ☆ ☆
_____	☆ ☆ ☆ ☆ ☆	_____	☆ ☆ ☆ ☆ ☆
_____	☆ ☆ ☆ ☆ ☆	_____	☆ ☆ ☆ ☆ ☆

TRIP MEMORIES & OTHER NOTES:

NATIONAL PARK TRIP PLANNER:

City: _____   **State:** _____

Trip Start/End Date: _____

Anticipated Weather:

ACCOMMODATIONS: _____

PHONE: _____   PARK CELL RECEPTION ☐

PETS ALLOWED: ☐   PARK WIFI: ☐

SUPPLIES:

TO DO:

- ☐ LODGING RESERVATIONS
- ☐ PARK ENTRANCE PASS
- ☐ NATIONAL PARK/FED LANDS PASS
- ☐ TRIP PLAN FOR EMERGENCY CONTACT
- ☐ SAFETY LEADER: _____
- ☐ VEHICLE REGISTERED, IF REQUIRED
- ☐ DOWNLOAD NATIONAL PARK APP
- ☐ SAVED PARK FOR OFFLINE USE
- ☐ PACKED THE 10 ESSENTIALS
- ☐
- ☐
- ☐

PARK FEES

PARK ENTRANCE: _____

LODGING PER NIGHT: _____

VEHICLE REGISTRATION: _____

OTHER FEES: _____

_____

_____

ACTIVITY & PLACES TO VISIT ITINERARY

DATE/TIME	ACTIVITY	RESERVATIONS

OTHER NOTES:

NATIONAL PARK:

Overall Rating ☆ ☆ ☆ ☆ ☆

FAVORITE ACTIVITY:_____

FAVORITE TRAIL:_____

TOP WILDLIFE SIGHTS:_____

BEST SCENIC VIEWS_____

ACTIVITY ☆ ☆ ☆ ☆ ☆

LODGING ☆ ☆ ☆ ☆ ☆

FLORA & FAUNA ☆ ☆ ☆ ☆ ☆

CROWDS ☆ ☆ ☆ ☆ ☆

STARGAZING ☆ ☆ ☆ ☆ ☆

PASSPORT STAMP & MEMORABILIA

TO REMEMBER OR DO NEXT VISIT

ACTIVITY & RATING

_____	☆ ☆ ☆ ☆ ☆	_____	☆ ☆ ☆ ☆ ☆
_____	☆ ☆ ☆ ☆ ☆	_____	☆ ☆ ☆ ☆ ☆
_____	☆ ☆ ☆ ☆ ☆	_____	☆ ☆ ☆ ☆ ☆
_____	☆ ☆ ☆ ☆ ☆	_____	☆ ☆ ☆ ☆ ☆
_____	☆ ☆ ☆ ☆ ☆	_____	☆ ☆ ☆ ☆ ☆
_____	☆ ☆ ☆ ☆ ☆	_____	☆ ☆ ☆ ☆ ☆
_____	☆ ☆ ☆ ☆ ☆	_____	☆ ☆ ☆ ☆ ☆
_____	☆ ☆ ☆ ☆ ☆	_____	☆ ☆ ☆ ☆ ☆

TRIP MEMORIES & OTHER NOTES:

NATIONAL PARK TRIP PLANNER:

City: _____ **State:** _____ **Anticipated Weather:**

Trip Start/End Date: _____

ACCOMMODATIONS: _____

PHONE: _____ PARK CELL RECEPTION ☐

PETS ALLOWED: ☐ PARK WIFI: ☐

SUPPLIES:

TO DO:

☐ LODGING RESERVATIONS
☐ PARK ENTRANCE PASS
☐ NATIONAL PARK/FED LANDS PASS
☐ TRIP PLAN FOR EMERGENCY
  CONTACT
☐ SAFETY LEADER: _____
☐ VEHICLE REGISTERED, IF
  REQUIRED
☐ DOWNLOAD NATIONAL PARK APP
☐ SAVED PARK FOR OFFLINE USE
☐ PACKED THE 10 ESSENTIALS
☐
☐
☐

PARK FEES

PARK ENTRANCE: _____

LODGING PER NIGHT: _____

VEHICLE REGISTRATION: _____

OTHER FEES: _____

_____

_____

ACTIVITY & PLACES TO VISIT ITINERARY

DATE/TIME	ACTIVITY	RESERVATIONS

OTHER NOTES:

NATIONAL PARK:

Overall Rating ☆ ☆ ☆ ☆ ☆

FAVORITE ACTIVITY:_____

FAVORITE TRAIL:_____

TOP WILDLIFE SIGHTS:_____

BEST SCENIC VIEWS_____

ACTIVITY ☆ ☆ ☆ ☆ ☆

LODGING ☆ ☆ ☆ ☆ ☆

FLORA & FAUNA ☆ ☆ ☆ ☆ ☆

CROWDS ☆ ☆ ☆ ☆ ☆

STARGAZING ☆ ☆ ☆ ☆ ☆

PASSPORT STAMP & MEMORABILIA

TO REMEMBER OR DO NEXT VISIT

ACTIVITY & RATING

_____	☆ ☆ ☆ ☆ ☆	_____	☆ ☆ ☆ ☆ ☆
_____	☆ ☆ ☆ ☆ ☆	_____	☆ ☆ ☆ ☆ ☆
_____	☆ ☆ ☆ ☆ ☆	_____	☆ ☆ ☆ ☆ ☆
_____	☆ ☆ ☆ ☆ ☆	_____	☆ ☆ ☆ ☆ ☆
_____	☆ ☆ ☆ ☆ ☆	_____	☆ ☆ ☆ ☆ ☆
_____	☆ ☆ ☆ ☆ ☆	_____	☆ ☆ ☆ ☆ ☆
_____	☆ ☆ ☆ ☆ ☆	_____	☆ ☆ ☆ ☆ ☆
_____	☆ ☆ ☆ ☆ ☆	_____	☆ ☆ ☆ ☆ ☆

TRIP MEMORIES & OTHER NOTES:

NATIONAL PARK TRIP PLANNER:

City: _____ **State:** _____

Anticipated Weather:

Trip Start/End Date:_____

ACCOMMODATIONS: _____

PHONE: _____ PARK CELL RECEPTION ☐

PETS ALLOWED: ☐ PARK WIFI: ☐

SUPPLIES:

PARK FEES

PARK ENTRANCE:_____

LODGING PER NIGHT:_____

VEHICLE REGISTRATION: _____

OTHER FEES:_____

_____

_____

TO DO:

☐ LODGING RESERVATIONS

☐ PARK ENTRANCE PASS

☐ NATIONAL PARK/FED LANDS PASS

☐ TRIP PLAN FOR EMERGENCY
   CONTACT

☐ SAFETY LEADER: _____

☐ VEHICLE REGISTERED, IF
   REQUIRED

☐ DOWNLOAD NATIONAL PARK APP

☐ SAVED PARK FOR OFFLINE USE

☐ PACKED THE 10 ESSENTIALS

☐

☐

☐

ACTIVITY & PLACES TO VISIT ITINERARY

DATE/TIME	ACTIVITY	RESERVATIONS

OTHER NOTES:

NATIONAL PARK:

Overall Rating ☆ ☆ ☆ ☆ ☆

FAVORITE ACTIVITY:_____

FAVORITE TRAIL:_____

TOP WILDLIFE SIGHTS:_____

BEST SCENIC VIEWS_____

ACTIVITY ☆ ☆ ☆ ☆ ☆

LODGING ☆ ☆ ☆ ☆ ☆

FLORA & FAUNA ☆ ☆ ☆ ☆ ☆

CROWDS ☆ ☆ ☆ ☆ ☆

STARGAZING ☆ ☆ ☆ ☆ ☆

PASSPORT STAMP & MEMORABILIA

TO REMEMBER OR DO NEXT VISIT

ACTIVITY & RATING

_____	☆ ☆ ☆ ☆ ☆	_____	☆ ☆ ☆ ☆ ☆
_____	☆ ☆ ☆ ☆ ☆	_____	☆ ☆ ☆ ☆ ☆
_____	☆ ☆ ☆ ☆ ☆	_____	☆ ☆ ☆ ☆ ☆
_____	☆ ☆ ☆ ☆ ☆	_____	☆ ☆ ☆ ☆ ☆
_____	☆ ☆ ☆ ☆ ☆	_____	☆ ☆ ☆ ☆ ☆
_____	☆ ☆ ☆ ☆ ☆	_____	☆ ☆ ☆ ☆ ☆
_____	☆ ☆ ☆ ☆ ☆	_____	☆ ☆ ☆ ☆ ☆
_____	☆ ☆ ☆ ☆ ☆	_____	☆ ☆ ☆ ☆ ☆

TRIP MEMORIES & OTHER NOTES:

NATIONAL PARK TRIP PLANNER:

City: _____ **State:** _____

Anticipated Weather:

Trip Start/End Date: _____

☀ ⛅ 🌤 🌦 🌧 ☁ 🌥 🌦

ACCOMMODATIONS: _____

PHONE: _____   PARK CELL RECEPTION ☐

PETS ALLOWED: ☐   PARK WIFI: ☐

SUPPLIES:

PARK FEES

PARK ENTRANCE: _____

LODGING PER NIGHT: _____

VEHICLE REGISTRATION: _____

OTHER FEES: _____

_____

_____

TO DO:

- ☐ LODGING RESERVATIONS
- ☐ PARK ENTRANCE PASS
- ☐ NATIONAL PARK/FED LANDS PASS
- ☐ TRIP PLAN FOR EMERGENCY CONTACT
- ☐ SAFETY LEADER: _____
- ☐ VEHICLE REGISTERED, IF REQUIRED
- ☐ DOWNLOAD NATIONAL PARK APP
- ☐ SAVED PARK FOR OFFLINE USE
- ☐ PACKED THE 10 ESSENTIALS
- ☐
- ☐
- ☐

ACTIVITY & PLACES TO VISIT ITINERARY

DATE/TIME	ACTIVITY	RESERVATIONS

OTHER NOTES:

NATIONAL PARK:

Overall Rating ☆ ☆ ☆ ☆ ☆

FAVORITE ACTIVITY:_____

FAVORITE TRAIL:_____

TOP WILDLIFE SIGHTS:_____

BEST SCENIC VIEWS_____

ACTIVITY ☆ ☆ ☆ ☆ ☆

LODGING ☆ ☆ ☆ ☆ ☆

FLORA & FAUNA ☆ ☆ ☆ ☆ ☆

CROWDS ☆ ☆ ☆ ☆ ☆

STARGAZING ☆ ☆ ☆ ☆ ☆

PASSPORT STAMP & MEMORABILIA

TO REMEMBER OR DO NEXT VISIT

ACTIVITY & RATING

_____	☆ ☆ ☆ ☆ ☆	_____	☆ ☆ ☆ ☆ ☆
_____	☆ ☆ ☆ ☆ ☆	_____	☆ ☆ ☆ ☆ ☆
_____	☆ ☆ ☆ ☆ ☆	_____	☆ ☆ ☆ ☆ ☆
_____	☆ ☆ ☆ ☆ ☆	_____	☆ ☆ ☆ ☆ ☆
_____	☆ ☆ ☆ ☆ ☆	_____	☆ ☆ ☆ ☆ ☆
_____	☆ ☆ ☆ ☆ ☆	_____	☆ ☆ ☆ ☆ ☆
_____	☆ ☆ ☆ ☆ ☆	_____	☆ ☆ ☆ ☆ ☆
	☆ ☆ ☆ ☆ ☆		☆ ☆ ☆ ☆ ☆

TRIP MEMORIES & OTHER NOTES:

National Park Trip Planner:

City: _____ **State:** _____

Anticipated Weather:

Trip Start/End Date:_____

ACCOMMODATIONS: _____

PHONE: _____   PARK CELL RECEPTION ☐

PETS ALLOWED: ☐   PARK WIFI: ☐

SUPPLIES:

PARK FEES

PARK ENTRANCE:_____

LODGING PER NIGHT:_____

VEHICLE REGISTRATION: _____

OTHER FEES:_____

_____

_____

TO DO:

☐ LODGING RESERVATIONS

☐ PARK ENTRANCE PASS

☐ NATIONAL PARK/FED LANDS PASS

☐ TRIP PLAN FOR EMERGENCY CONTACT

☐ SAFETY LEADER: _____

☐ VEHICLE REGISTERED, IF REQUIRED

☐ DOWNLOAD NATIONAL PARK APP

☐ SAVED PARK FOR OFFLINE USE

☐ PACKED THE 10 ESSENTIALS

☐

☐

☐

ACTIVITY & PLACES TO VISIT ITINERARY

DATE/TIME	ACTIVITY	RESERVATIONS

OTHER NOTES:

NATIONAL PARK:

Overall Rating ☆ ☆ ☆ ☆ ☆

FAVORITE ACTIVITY:_____

FAVORITE TRAIL:_____

TOP WILDLIFE SIGHTS:_____

BEST SCENIC VIEWS_____

ACTIVITY ☆ ☆ ☆ ☆ ☆

LODGING ☆ ☆ ☆ ☆ ☆

FLORA & FAUNA ☆ ☆ ☆ ☆ ☆

CROWDS ☆ ☆ ☆ ☆ ☆

STARGAZING ☆ ☆ ☆ ☆ ☆

PASSPORT STAMP & MEMORABILIA

TO REMEMBER OR DO NEXT VISIT

ACTIVITY & RATING

_____	☆ ☆ ☆ ☆ ☆	_____	☆ ☆ ☆ ☆ ☆
_____	☆ ☆ ☆ ☆ ☆	_____	☆ ☆ ☆ ☆ ☆
_____	☆ ☆ ☆ ☆ ☆	_____	☆ ☆ ☆ ☆ ☆
_____	☆ ☆ ☆ ☆ ☆	_____	☆ ☆ ☆ ☆ ☆
_____	☆ ☆ ☆ ☆ ☆	_____	☆ ☆ ☆ ☆ ☆
_____	☆ ☆ ☆ ☆ ☆	_____	☆ ☆ ☆ ☆ ☆
_____	☆ ☆ ☆ ☆ ☆	_____	☆ ☆ ☆ ☆ ☆
_____	☆ ☆ ☆ ☆ ☆	_____	☆ ☆ ☆ ☆ ☆

TRIP MEMORIES & OTHER NOTES:

NATIONAL PARK TRIP PLANNER:

City: _____ **State:** _____

Anticipated Weather:

Trip Start/End Date: _____

ACCOMMODATIONS: _____

PHONE: _____

PARK CELL RECEPTION ☐

PETS ALLOWED: ☐

PARK WIFI: ☐

SUPPLIES:

TO DO:

- ☐ LODGING RESERVATIONS
- ☐ PARK ENTRANCE PASS
- ☐ NATIONAL PARK/FED LANDS PASS
- ☐ TRIP PLAN FOR EMERGENCY CONTACT
- ☐ SAFETY LEADER: _____
- ☐ VEHICLE REGISTERED, IF REQUIRED
- ☐ DOWNLOAD NATIONAL PARK APP
- ☐ SAVED PARK FOR OFFLINE USE
- ☐ PACKED THE 10 ESSENTIALS
- ☐
- ☐
- ☐

PARK FEES

PARK ENTRANCE: _____

LODGING PER NIGHT: _____

VEHICLE REGISTRATION: _____

OTHER FEES: _____

_____

_____

ACTIVITY & PLACES TO VISIT ITINERARY

DATE/TIME	ACTIVITY	RESERVATIONS

OTHER NOTES:

NATIONAL PARK:

Overall Rating ☆ ☆ ☆ ☆ ☆

FAVORITE ACTIVITY:_____

FAVORITE TRAIL:_____

TOP WILDLIFE SIGHTS:_____

BEST SCENIC VIEWS_____

ACTIVITY ☆ ☆ ☆ ☆ ☆

LODGING ☆ ☆ ☆ ☆ ☆

FLORA & FAUNA ☆ ☆ ☆ ☆ ☆

CROWDS ☆ ☆ ☆ ☆ ☆

STARGAZING ☆ ☆ ☆ ☆ ☆

PASSPORT STAMP & MEMORABILIA

TO REMEMBER OR DO NEXT VISIT

ACTIVITY & RATING

_____	☆ ☆ ☆ ☆ ☆	_____	☆ ☆ ☆ ☆ ☆
_____	☆ ☆ ☆ ☆ ☆	_____	☆ ☆ ☆ ☆ ☆
_____	☆ ☆ ☆ ☆ ☆	_____	☆ ☆ ☆ ☆ ☆
_____	☆ ☆ ☆ ☆ ☆	_____	☆ ☆ ☆ ☆ ☆
_____	☆ ☆ ☆ ☆ ☆	_____	☆ ☆ ☆ ☆ ☆
_____	☆ ☆ ☆ ☆ ☆	_____	☆ ☆ ☆ ☆ ☆
_____	☆ ☆ ☆ ☆ ☆	_____	☆ ☆ ☆ ☆ ☆
_____	☆ ☆ ☆ ☆ ☆	_____	☆ ☆ ☆ ☆ ☆

TRIP MEMORIES & OTHER NOTES:

NATIONAL PARK TRIP PLANNER:

City: _____ **State:** _____

Anticipated Weather:

Trip Start/End Date: _____

ACCOMMODATIONS: _____

PHONE: _____   PARK CELL RECEPTION ☐

PETS ALLOWED: ☐   PARK WIFI: ☐

SUPPLIES:

TO DO:

☐ LODGING RESERVATIONS
☐ PARK ENTRANCE PASS
☐ NATIONAL PARK/FED LANDS PASS
☐ TRIP PLAN FOR EMERGENCY
   CONTACT
☐ SAFETY LEADER: _____

PARK FEES

PARK ENTRANCE: _____

LODGING PER NIGHT: _____

VEHICLE REGISTRATION: _____

OTHER FEES: _____

_____

_____

☐ VEHICLE REGISTERED, IF
   REQUIRED
☐ DOWNLOAD NATIONAL PARK APP
☐ SAVED PARK FOR OFFLINE USE
☐ PACKED THE 10 ESSENTIALS
☐
☐
☐

ACTIVITY & PLACES TO VISIT ITINERARY

DATE/TIME	ACTIVITY	RESERVATIONS

OTHER NOTES:

NATIONAL PARK:

Overall Rating ☆ ☆ ☆ ☆ ☆

FAVORITE ACTIVITY: _____

FAVORITE TRAIL: _____

TOP WILDLIFE SIGHTS: _____

BEST SCENIC VIEWS _____

ACTIVITY ☆ ☆ ☆ ☆ ☆

LODGING ☆ ☆ ☆ ☆ ☆

FLORA & FAUNA ☆ ☆ ☆ ☆ ☆

CROWDS ☆ ☆ ☆ ☆ ☆

STARGAZING ☆ ☆ ☆ ☆ ☆

PASSPORT STAMP & MEMORABILIA

TO REMEMBER OR DO NEXT VISIT

ACTIVITY & RATING

_____	☆ ☆ ☆ ☆ ☆	_____	☆ ☆ ☆ ☆ ☆
_____	☆ ☆ ☆ ☆ ☆	_____	☆ ☆ ☆ ☆ ☆
_____	☆ ☆ ☆ ☆ ☆	_____	☆ ☆ ☆ ☆ ☆
_____	☆ ☆ ☆ ☆ ☆	_____	☆ ☆ ☆ ☆ ☆
_____	☆ ☆ ☆ ☆ ☆	_____	☆ ☆ ☆ ☆ ☆
_____	☆ ☆ ☆ ☆ ☆	_____	☆ ☆ ☆ ☆ ☆
_____	☆ ☆ ☆ ☆ ☆	_____	☆ ☆ ☆ ☆ ☆
_____	☆ ☆ ☆ ☆ ☆	_____	☆ ☆ ☆ ☆ ☆

TRIP MEMORIES & OTHER NOTES:

NATIONAL PARK TRIP PLANNER:

City: _____ **State:** _____

Trip Start/End Date: _____

Anticipated Weather:

ACCOMMODATIONS: _____

PHONE: _____   PARK CELL RECEPTION ☐

PETS ALLOWED: ☐   PARK WIFI: ☐

SUPPLIES:

TO DO:

☐ LODGING RESERVATIONS
☐ PARK ENTRANCE PASS
☐ NATIONAL PARK/FED LANDS PASS
☐ TRIP PLAN FOR EMERGENCY
   CONTACT
☐ SAFETY LEADER: _____

PARK FEES

PARK ENTRANCE: _____

LODGING PER NIGHT: _____

VEHICLE REGISTRATION: _____

OTHER FEES: _____

_____

_____

☐ VEHICLE REGISTERED, IF
   REQUIRED
☐ DOWNLOAD NATIONAL PARK APP
☐ SAVED PARK FOR OFFLINE USE
☐ PACKED THE 10 ESSENTIALS
☐
☐
☐

ACTIVITY & PLACES TO VISIT ITINERARY

DATE/TIME	ACTIVITY	RESERVATIONS

OTHER NOTES:

NATIONAL PARK:

Overall Rating ☆ ☆ ☆ ☆ ☆

FAVORITE ACTIVITY:_____

FAVORITE TRAIL:_____

TOP WILDLIFE SIGHTS:_____

BEST SCENIC VIEWS_____

ACTIVITY ☆ ☆ ☆ ☆ ☆

LODGING ☆ ☆ ☆ ☆ ☆

FLORA & FAUNA ☆ ☆ ☆ ☆ ☆

CROWDS ☆ ☆ ☆ ☆ ☆

STARGAZING ☆ ☆ ☆ ☆ ☆

PASSPORT STAMP & MEMORABILIA

TO REMEMBER OR DO NEXT VISIT

ACTIVITY & RATING

_____	☆ ☆ ☆ ☆ ☆	_____	☆ ☆ ☆ ☆ ☆
_____	☆ ☆ ☆ ☆ ☆	_____	☆ ☆ ☆ ☆ ☆
_____	☆ ☆ ☆ ☆ ☆	_____	☆ ☆ ☆ ☆ ☆
_____	☆ ☆ ☆ ☆ ☆	_____	☆ ☆ ☆ ☆ ☆
_____	☆ ☆ ☆ ☆ ☆	_____	☆ ☆ ☆ ☆ ☆
_____	☆ ☆ ☆ ☆ ☆	_____	☆ ☆ ☆ ☆ ☆
_____	☆ ☆ ☆ ☆ ☆	_____	☆ ☆ ☆ ☆ ☆
_____	☆ ☆ ☆ ☆ ☆	_____	☆ ☆ ☆ ☆ ☆

TRIP MEMORIES & OTHER NOTES:

NATIONAL PARK TRIP PLANNER:

City: _____ **State:** _____

Trip Start/End Date: _____

Anticipated Weather:

ACCOMMODATIONS: _____

PHONE: _____

PETS ALLOWED: ☐

PARK CELL RECEPTION ☐

PARK WIFI: ☐

SUPPLIES:

TO DO:

☐ LODGING RESERVATIONS
☐ PARK ENTRANCE PASS
☐ NATIONAL PARK/FED LANDS PASS
☐ TRIP PLAN FOR EMERGENCY CONTACT
☐ SAFETY LEADER: _____
☐ VEHICLE REGISTERED, IF REQUIRED
☐ DOWNLOAD NATIONAL PARK APP
☐ SAVED PARK FOR OFFLINE USE
☐ PACKED THE 10 ESSENTIALS
☐
☐
☐

PARK FEES

PARK ENTRANCE: _____

LODGING PER NIGHT: _____

VEHICLE REGISTRATION: _____

OTHER FEES: _____

_____

_____

ACTIVITY & PLACES TO VISIT ITINERARY

DATE/TIME	ACTIVITY	RESERVATIONS

OTHER NOTES:

NATIONAL PARK:

Overall Rating ☆ ☆ ☆ ☆ ☆

FAVORITE ACTIVITY:_____

FAVORITE TRAIL:_____

TOP WILDLIFE SIGHTS:_____

BEST SCENIC VIEWS_____

ACTIVITY ☆ ☆ ☆ ☆ ☆

LODGING ☆ ☆ ☆ ☆ ☆

FLORA & FAUNA ☆ ☆ ☆ ☆ ☆

CROWDS ☆ ☆ ☆ ☆ ☆

STARGAZING ☆ ☆ ☆ ☆ ☆

PASSPORT STAMP & MEMORABILIA

TO REMEMBER OR DO NEXT VISIT

ACTIVITY & RATING

_____	☆ ☆ ☆ ☆ ☆	_____	☆ ☆ ☆ ☆ ☆
_____	☆ ☆ ☆ ☆ ☆	_____	☆ ☆ ☆ ☆ ☆
_____	☆ ☆ ☆ ☆ ☆	_____	☆ ☆ ☆ ☆ ☆
_____	☆ ☆ ☆ ☆ ☆	_____	☆ ☆ ☆ ☆ ☆
_____	☆ ☆ ☆ ☆ ☆	_____	☆ ☆ ☆ ☆ ☆
_____	☆ ☆ ☆ ☆ ☆	_____	☆ ☆ ☆ ☆ ☆
_____	☆ ☆ ☆ ☆ ☆	_____	☆ ☆ ☆ ☆ ☆
☆ ☆ ☆ ☆ ☆			☆ ☆ ☆ ☆ ☆

TRIP MEMORIES & OTHER NOTES:

NATIONAL PARK TRIP PLANNER:

City: _____ **State:** _____ **Anticipated Weather:**

Trip Start/End Date:_____

ACCOMMODATIONS: _____

PHONE: _____ PARK CELL RECEPTION ☐

PETS ALLOWED: ☐ PARK WIFI: ☐

SUPPLIES:

TO DO:

☐ LODGING RESERVATIONS
☐ PARK ENTRANCE PASS
☐ NATIONAL PARK/FED LANDS PASS
☐ TRIP PLAN FOR EMERGENCY
  CONTACT
☐ SAFETY LEADER: _____
☐ VEHICLE REGISTERED, IF
  REQUIRED
☐ DOWNLOAD NATIONAL PARK APP
☐ SAVED PARK FOR OFFLINE USE
☐ PACKED THE 10 ESSENTIALS
☐
☐
☐

PARK FEES

PARK ENTRANCE: _____
LODGING PER NIGHT: _____
VEHICLE REGISTRATION: _____
OTHER FEES: _____
_____
_____

ACTIVITY & PLACES TO VISIT ITINERARY

DATE/TIME	ACTIVITY	RESERVATIONS

OTHER NOTES:

NATIONAL PARK:

Overall Rating ☆ ☆ ☆ ☆ ☆

FAVORITE ACTIVITY:_____

FAVORITE TRAIL:_____

TOP WILDLIFE SIGHTS:_____

BEST SCENIC VIEWS_____

ACTIVITY ☆ ☆ ☆ ☆ ☆

LODGING ☆ ☆ ☆ ☆ ☆

FLORA & FAUNA ☆ ☆ ☆ ☆ ☆

CROWDS ☆ ☆ ☆ ☆ ☆

STARGAZING ☆ ☆ ☆ ☆ ☆

PASSPORT STAMP & MEMORABILIA

TO REMEMBER OR DO NEXT VISIT

ACTIVITY & RATING

_____	☆ ☆ ☆ ☆ ☆	_____	☆ ☆ ☆ ☆ ☆
_____	☆ ☆ ☆ ☆ ☆	_____	☆ ☆ ☆ ☆ ☆
_____	☆ ☆ ☆ ☆ ☆	_____	☆ ☆ ☆ ☆ ☆
_____	☆ ☆ ☆ ☆ ☆	_____	☆ ☆ ☆ ☆ ☆
_____	☆ ☆ ☆ ☆ ☆	_____	☆ ☆ ☆ ☆ ☆
_____	☆ ☆ ☆ ☆ ☆	_____	☆ ☆ ☆ ☆ ☆
_____	☆ ☆ ☆ ☆ ☆	_____	☆ ☆ ☆ ☆ ☆
	☆ ☆ ☆ ☆ ☆		☆ ☆ ☆ ☆ ☆

TRIP MEMORIES & OTHER NOTES:

National Park Trip Planner:

City: _____ **State:** _____

Trip Start/End Date: _____

Anticipated Weather:

ACCOMMODATIONS: _____

PHONE: _____   PARK CELL RECEPTION ☐

PETS ALLOWED: ☐   PARK WIFI: ☐

SUPPLIES:

PARK FEES

PARK ENTRANCE: _____

LODGING PER NIGHT: _____

VEHICLE REGISTRATION: _____

OTHER FEES: _____

_____

_____

TO DO:

☐ LODGING RESERVATIONS
☐ PARK ENTRANCE PASS
☐ NATIONAL PARK/FED LANDS PASS
☐ TRIP PLAN FOR EMERGENCY
   CONTACT
☐ SAFETY LEADER: _____
☐ VEHICLE REGISTERED, IF
   REQUIRED
☐ DOWNLOAD NATIONAL PARK APP
☐ SAVED PARK FOR OFFLINE USE
☐ PACKED THE 10 ESSENTIALS
☐
☐
☐

ACTIVITY & PLACES TO VISIT ITINERARY

DATE/TIME	ACTIVITY	RESERVATIONS

OTHER NOTES:

NATIONAL PARK:

Overall Rating ☆ ☆ ☆ ☆ ☆

FAVORITE ACTIVITY:_____

FAVORITE TRAIL:_____

TOP WILDLIFE SIGHTS:_____

BEST SCENIC VIEWS_____

ACTIVITY ☆ ☆ ☆ ☆ ☆

LODGING ☆ ☆ ☆ ☆ ☆

FLORA & FAUNA ☆ ☆ ☆ ☆ ☆

CROWDS ☆ ☆ ☆ ☆ ☆

STARGAZING ☆ ☆ ☆ ☆ ☆

PASSPORT STAMP & MEMORABILIA

TO REMEMBER OR DO NEXT VISIT

ACTIVITY & RATING

_____	☆ ☆ ☆ ☆ ☆	_____	☆ ☆ ☆ ☆ ☆
_____	☆ ☆ ☆ ☆ ☆	_____	☆ ☆ ☆ ☆ ☆
_____	☆ ☆ ☆ ☆ ☆	_____	☆ ☆ ☆ ☆ ☆
_____	☆ ☆ ☆ ☆ ☆	_____	☆ ☆ ☆ ☆ ☆
_____	☆ ☆ ☆ ☆ ☆	_____	☆ ☆ ☆ ☆ ☆
_____	☆ ☆ ☆ ☆ ☆	_____	☆ ☆ ☆ ☆ ☆
_____	☆ ☆ ☆ ☆ ☆	_____	☆ ☆ ☆ ☆ ☆
_____	☆ ☆ ☆ ☆ ☆	_____	☆ ☆ ☆ ☆ ☆

TRIP MEMORIES & OTHER NOTES:

NATIONAL PARK TRIP PLANNER:

City: **State:**

Trip Start/End Date:_____

Anticipated Weather:

ACCOMMODATIONS: _____

PHONE: _____   PARK CELL RECEPTION ☐

PETS ALLOWED: ☐   PARK WIFI: ☐

SUPPLIES:

PARK FEES

PARK ENTRANCE: _____

LODGING PER NIGHT: _____

VEHICLE REGISTRATION: _____

OTHER FEES: _____

_____

_____

TO DO:

☐ LODGING RESERVATIONS
☐ PARK ENTRANCE PASS
☐ NATIONAL PARK/FED LANDS PASS
☐ TRIP PLAN FOR EMERGENCY
  CONTACT
☐ SAFETY LEADER: _____
☐ VEHICLE REGISTERED, IF
  REQUIRED
☐ DOWNLOAD NATIONAL PARK APP
☐ SAVED PARK FOR OFFLINE USE
☐ PACKED THE 10 ESSENTIALS
☐
☐
☐

ACTIVITY & PLACES TO VISIT ITINERARY

DATE/TIME	ACTIVITY	RESERVATIONS

OTHER NOTES:

NATIONAL PARK:

Overall Rating ☆ ☆ ☆ ☆ ☆

FAVORITE ACTIVITY:_____

FAVORITE TRAIL:_____

TOP WILDLIFE SIGHTS:_____

BEST SCENIC VIEWS_____

ACTIVITY ☆ ☆ ☆ ☆ ☆

LODGING ☆ ☆ ☆ ☆ ☆

FLORA & FAUNA ☆ ☆ ☆ ☆ ☆

CROWDS ☆ ☆ ☆ ☆ ☆

STARGAZING ☆ ☆ ☆ ☆ ☆

PASSPORT STAMP & MEMORABILIA

TO REMEMBER OR DO NEXT VISIT

ACTIVITY & RATING

_____	☆ ☆ ☆ ☆ ☆	_____	☆ ☆ ☆ ☆ ☆
_____	☆ ☆ ☆ ☆ ☆	_____	☆ ☆ ☆ ☆ ☆
_____	☆ ☆ ☆ ☆ ☆	_____	☆ ☆ ☆ ☆ ☆
_____	☆ ☆ ☆ ☆ ☆	_____	☆ ☆ ☆ ☆ ☆
_____	☆ ☆ ☆ ☆ ☆	_____	☆ ☆ ☆ ☆ ☆
_____	☆ ☆ ☆ ☆ ☆	_____	☆ ☆ ☆ ☆ ☆
_____	☆ ☆ ☆ ☆ ☆	_____	☆ ☆ ☆ ☆ ☆
_____	☆ ☆ ☆ ☆ ☆	_____	☆ ☆ ☆ ☆ ☆

TRIP MEMORIES & OTHER NOTES:

NATIONAL PARK TRIP PLANNER:

City: _____ **State:** _____

Anticipated Weather:

Trip Start/End Date:_____

ACCOMMODATIONS: _____

PHONE: _____ PARK CELL RECEPTION ☐

PETS ALLOWED: ☐ PARK WIFI: ☐

SUPPLIES:

TO DO:

☐ LODGING RESERVATIONS
☐ PARK ENTRANCE PASS
☐ NATIONAL PARK/FED LANDS PASS
☐ TRIP PLAN FOR EMERGENCY
   CONTACT
☐ SAFETY LEADER: _____

PARK FEES

PARK ENTRANCE:_____

LODGING PER NIGHT:_____

VEHICLE REGISTRATION: _____

OTHER FEES:_____

_____

_____

☐ VEHICLE REGISTERED, IF
   REQUIRED
☐ DOWNLOAD NATIONAL PARK APP
☐ SAVED PARK FOR OFFLINE USE
☐ PACKED THE 10 ESSENTIALS
☐
☐
☐

ACTIVITY & PLACES TO VISIT ITINERARY

DATE/TIME	ACTIVITY	RESERVATIONS

OTHER NOTES:

NATIONAL PARK:

Overall Rating ☆ ☆ ☆ ☆ ☆

FAVORITE ACTIVITY:_____

FAVORITE TRAIL:_____

TOP WILDLIFE SIGHTS:_____

BEST SCENIC VIEWS_____

ACTIVITY ☆ ☆ ☆ ☆ ☆

LODGING ☆ ☆ ☆ ☆ ☆

FLORA & FAUNA ☆ ☆ ☆ ☆ ☆

CROWDS ☆ ☆ ☆ ☆ ☆

STARGAZING ☆ ☆ ☆ ☆ ☆

PASSPORT STAMP & MEMORABILIA

TO REMEMBER OR DO NEXT VISIT

ACTIVITY & RATING

_____	☆ ☆ ☆ ☆ ☆	_____	☆ ☆ ☆ ☆ ☆
_____	☆ ☆ ☆ ☆ ☆	_____	☆ ☆ ☆ ☆ ☆
_____	☆ ☆ ☆ ☆ ☆	_____	☆ ☆ ☆ ☆ ☆
_____	☆ ☆ ☆ ☆ ☆	_____	☆ ☆ ☆ ☆ ☆
_____	☆ ☆ ☆ ☆ ☆	_____	☆ ☆ ☆ ☆ ☆
_____	☆ ☆ ☆ ☆ ☆	_____	☆ ☆ ☆ ☆ ☆
_____	☆ ☆ ☆ ☆ ☆	_____	☆ ☆ ☆ ☆ ☆
_____	☆ ☆ ☆ ☆ ☆	_____	☆ ☆ ☆ ☆ ☆

TRIP MEMORIES & OTHER NOTES:

National Park Trip Planner:

City: **State:**

Trip Start/End Date:_____

Anticipated Weather:

ACCOMMODATIONS: _____

PHONE: _____   PARK CELL RECEPTION ☐

PETS ALLOWED: ☐   PARK WIFI: ☐

SUPPLIES:

PARK FEES

PARK ENTRANCE: _____

LODGING PER NIGHT: _____

VEHICLE REGISTRATION: _____

OTHER FEES: _____

_____

_____

TO DO:

☐ LODGING RESERVATIONS

☐ PARK ENTRANCE PASS

☐ NATIONAL PARK/FED LANDS PASS

☐ TRIP PLAN FOR EMERGENCY CONTACT

☐ SAFETY LEADER: _____

☐ VEHICLE REGISTERED, IF REQUIRED

☐ DOWNLOAD NATIONAL PARK APP

☐ SAVED PARK FOR OFFLINE USE

☐ PACKED THE 10 ESSENTIALS

☐

☐

☐

ACTIVITY & PLACES TO VISIT ITINERARY

DATE/TIME	ACTIVITY	RESERVATIONS

OTHER NOTES:

NATIONAL PARK:

Overall Rating ☆ ☆ ☆ ☆ ☆

FAVORITE ACTIVITY:_____

FAVORITE TRAIL:_____

TOP WILDLIFE SIGHTS:_____

BEST SCENIC VIEWS_____

ACTIVITY ☆ ☆ ☆ ☆ ☆

LODGING ☆ ☆ ☆ ☆ ☆

FLORA & FAUNA ☆ ☆ ☆ ☆ ☆

CROWDS ☆ ☆ ☆ ☆ ☆

STARGAZING ☆ ☆ ☆ ☆ ☆

PASSPORT STAMP & MEMORABILIA

TO REMEMBER OR DO NEXT VISIT

ACTIVITY & RATING

_____	☆ ☆ ☆ ☆ ☆	_____	☆ ☆ ☆ ☆ ☆
_____	☆ ☆ ☆ ☆ ☆	_____	☆ ☆ ☆ ☆ ☆
_____	☆ ☆ ☆ ☆ ☆	_____	☆ ☆ ☆ ☆ ☆
_____	☆ ☆ ☆ ☆ ☆	_____	☆ ☆ ☆ ☆ ☆
_____	☆ ☆ ☆ ☆ ☆	_____	☆ ☆ ☆ ☆ ☆
_____	☆ ☆ ☆ ☆ ☆	_____	☆ ☆ ☆ ☆ ☆
_____	☆ ☆ ☆ ☆ ☆	_____	☆ ☆ ☆ ☆ ☆
_____	☆ ☆ ☆ ☆ ☆	_____	☆ ☆ ☆ ☆ ☆

TRIP MEMORIES & OTHER NOTES:

National Park Trip Planner:

City: **State:** **Anticipated Weather:**

Trip Start/End Date:_____

ACCOMMODATIONS: _____

PHONE: _____ PARK CELL RECEPTION ☐

PETS ALLOWED: ☐ PARK WIFI: ☐

SUPPLIES:

PARK FEES

PARK ENTRANCE:_____

LODGING PER NIGHT:_____

VEHICLE REGISTRATION: _____

OTHER FEES:_____

_____

_____

TO DO:

☐ LODGING RESERVATIONS

☐ PARK ENTRANCE PASS

☐ NATIONAL PARK/FED LANDS PASS

☐ TRIP PLAN FOR EMERGENCY CONTACT

☐ SAFETY LEADER: _____

☐ VEHICLE REGISTERED, IF REQUIRED

☐ DOWNLOAD NATIONAL PARK APP

☐ SAVED PARK FOR OFFLINE USE

☐ PACKED THE 10 ESSENTIALS

☐

☐

☐

ACTIVITY & PLACES TO VISIT ITINERARY

DATE/TIME	ACTIVITY	RESERVATIONS

OTHER NOTES:

NATIONAL PARK:

Overall Rating ☆ ☆ ☆ ☆ ☆

FAVORITE ACTIVITY: _____

FAVORITE TRAIL: _____

TOP WILDLIFE SIGHTS: _____

BEST SCENIC VIEWS _____

ACTIVITY ☆ ☆ ☆ ☆ ☆

LODGING ☆ ☆ ☆ ☆ ☆

FLORA & FAUNA ☆ ☆ ☆ ☆ ☆

CROWDS ☆ ☆ ☆ ☆ ☆

STARGAZING ☆ ☆ ☆ ☆ ☆

PASSPORT STAMP & MEMORABILIA

TO REMEMBER OR DO NEXT VISIT

ACTIVITY & RATING

_____	☆ ☆ ☆ ☆ ☆	_____	☆ ☆ ☆ ☆ ☆
_____	☆ ☆ ☆ ☆ ☆	_____	☆ ☆ ☆ ☆ ☆
_____	☆ ☆ ☆ ☆ ☆	_____	☆ ☆ ☆ ☆ ☆
_____	☆ ☆ ☆ ☆ ☆	_____	☆ ☆ ☆ ☆ ☆
_____	☆ ☆ ☆ ☆ ☆	_____	☆ ☆ ☆ ☆ ☆
_____	☆ ☆ ☆ ☆ ☆	_____	☆ ☆ ☆ ☆ ☆
_____	☆ ☆ ☆ ☆ ☆	_____	☆ ☆ ☆ ☆ ☆
_____	☆ ☆ ☆ ☆ ☆	_____	☆ ☆ ☆ ☆ ☆

TRIP MEMORIES & OTHER NOTES:

NATIONAL PARK TRIP PLANNER:

City: **State:**   **Anticipated Weather:**

Trip Start/End Date:_____

ACCOMMODATIONS: _____

PHONE: _____   PARK CELL RECEPTION ☐

PETS ALLOWED: ☐   PARK WIFI: ☐

SUPPLIES:

TO DO:

- ☐ LODGING RESERVATIONS
- ☐ PARK ENTRANCE PASS
- ☐ NATIONAL PARK/FED LANDS PASS
- ☐ TRIP PLAN FOR EMERGENCY CONTACT
- ☐ SAFETY LEADER: _____
- ☐ VEHICLE REGISTERED, IF REQUIRED
- ☐ DOWNLOAD NATIONAL PARK APP
- ☐ SAVED PARK FOR OFFLINE USE
- ☐ PACKED THE 10 ESSENTIALS
- ☐
- ☐
- ☐

PARK FEES

PARK ENTRANCE:_____

LODGING PER NIGHT:_____

VEHICLE REGISTRATION: _____

OTHER FEES:_____

_____

_____

ACTIVITY & PLACES TO VISIT ITINERARY

DATE/TIME	ACTIVITY	RESERVATIONS

OTHER NOTES:

NATIONAL PARK:

Overall Rating ☆ ☆ ☆ ☆ ☆

FAVORITE ACTIVITY:_____

FAVORITE TRAIL:_____

TOP WILDLIFE SIGHTS:_____

BEST SCENIC VIEWS_____

ACTIVITY ☆ ☆ ☆ ☆ ☆
LODGING ☆ ☆ ☆ ☆ ☆
FLORA & FAUNA ☆ ☆ ☆ ☆ ☆
CROWDS ☆ ☆ ☆ ☆ ☆
STARGAZING ☆ ☆ ☆ ☆ ☆

PASSPORT STAMP & MEMORABILIA

TO REMEMBER OR DO NEXT VISIT

ACTIVITY & RATING

_____	☆ ☆ ☆ ☆ ☆	_____	☆ ☆ ☆ ☆ ☆
_____	☆ ☆ ☆ ☆ ☆	_____	☆ ☆ ☆ ☆ ☆
_____	☆ ☆ ☆ ☆ ☆	_____	☆ ☆ ☆ ☆ ☆
_____	☆ ☆ ☆ ☆ ☆	_____	☆ ☆ ☆ ☆ ☆
_____	☆ ☆ ☆ ☆ ☆	_____	☆ ☆ ☆ ☆ ☆
_____	☆ ☆ ☆ ☆ ☆	_____	☆ ☆ ☆ ☆ ☆
_____	☆ ☆ ☆ ☆ ☆	_____	☆ ☆ ☆ ☆ ☆
	☆ ☆ ☆ ☆ ☆		☆ ☆ ☆ ☆ ☆

TRIP MEMORIES & OTHER NOTES:

NATIONAL PARK TRIP PLANNER:

City: _____ **State:** _____   **Anticipated Weather:**

Trip Start/End Date: _____

ACCOMMODATIONS: _____

PHONE: _____   PARK CELL RECEPTION ☐

PETS ALLOWED: ☐   PARK WIFI: ☐

SUPPLIES:

TO DO:

- ☐ LODGING RESERVATIONS
- ☐ PARK ENTRANCE PASS
- ☐ NATIONAL PARK/FED LANDS PASS
- ☐ TRIP PLAN FOR EMERGENCY CONTACT
- ☐ SAFETY LEADER: _____
- ☐ VEHICLE REGISTERED, IF REQUIRED
- ☐ DOWNLOAD NATIONAL PARK APP
- ☐ SAVED PARK FOR OFFLINE USE
- ☐ PACKED THE 10 ESSENTIALS
- ☐
- ☐
- ☐

PARK FEES

PARK ENTRANCE: _____

LODGING PER NIGHT: _____

VEHICLE REGISTRATION: _____

OTHER FEES: _____

_____

_____

ACTIVITY & PLACES TO VISIT ITINERARY

DATE/TIME	ACTIVITY	RESERVATIONS

OTHER NOTES:

NATIONAL PARK:

Overall Rating ☆ ☆ ☆ ☆ ☆

FAVORITE ACTIVITY:_____

FAVORITE TRAIL:_____

TOP WILDLIFE SIGHTS:_____

BEST SCENIC VIEWS_____

ACTIVITY ☆ ☆ ☆ ☆ ☆

LODGING ☆ ☆ ☆ ☆ ☆

FLORA & FAUNA ☆ ☆ ☆ ☆ ☆

CROWDS ☆ ☆ ☆ ☆ ☆

STARGAZING ☆ ☆ ☆ ☆ ☆

PASSPORT STAMP & MEMORABILIA

TO REMEMBER OR DO NEXT VISIT

ACTIVITY & RATING

_____	☆ ☆ ☆ ☆ ☆	_____	☆ ☆ ☆ ☆ ☆
_____	☆ ☆ ☆ ☆ ☆	_____	☆ ☆ ☆ ☆ ☆
_____	☆ ☆ ☆ ☆ ☆	_____	☆ ☆ ☆ ☆ ☆
_____	☆ ☆ ☆ ☆ ☆	_____	☆ ☆ ☆ ☆ ☆
_____	☆ ☆ ☆ ☆ ☆	_____	☆ ☆ ☆ ☆ ☆
_____	☆ ☆ ☆ ☆ ☆	_____	☆ ☆ ☆ ☆ ☆
_____	☆ ☆ ☆ ☆ ☆	_____	☆ ☆ ☆ ☆ ☆
_____	☆ ☆ ☆ ☆ ☆	_____	☆ ☆ ☆ ☆ ☆

TRIP MEMORIES & OTHER NOTES:

NATIONAL PARK TRIP PLANNER:

City: **State:**

Anticipated Weather:

Trip Start/End Date:_____

ACCOMMODATIONS: _____

PHONE: _____ PARK CELL RECEPTION ☐

PETS ALLOWED: ☐ PARK WIFI: ☐

SUPPLIES:

TO DO:

☐ LODGING RESERVATIONS
☐ PARK ENTRANCE PASS
☐ NATIONAL PARK/FED LANDS PASS
☐ TRIP PLAN FOR EMERGENCY
  CONTACT
☐ SAFETY LEADER: _____

PARK FEES

PARK ENTRANCE:_____

LODGING PER NIGHT:_____

VEHICLE REGISTRATION: _____

OTHER FEES:_____

_____

_____

☐ VEHICLE REGISTERED, IF
  REQUIRED
☐ DOWNLOAD NATIONAL PARK APP
☐ SAVED PARK FOR OFFLINE USE
☐ PACKED THE 10 ESSENTIALS
☐
☐
☐

ACTIVITY & PLACES TO VISIT ITINERARY

DATE/TIME	ACTIVITY	RESERVATIONS

OTHER NOTES:

NATIONAL PARK:

Overall Rating ☆ ☆ ☆ ☆ ☆

FAVORITE ACTIVITY:_____

FAVORITE TRAIL:_____

TOP WILDLIFE SIGHTS:_____

BEST SCENIC VIEWS_____

ACTIVITY ☆ ☆ ☆ ☆ ☆

LODGING ☆ ☆ ☆ ☆ ☆

FLORA & FAUNA ☆ ☆ ☆ ☆ ☆

CROWDS ☆ ☆ ☆ ☆ ☆

STARGAZING ☆ ☆ ☆ ☆ ☆

PASSPORT STAMP & MEMORABILIA

TO REMEMBER OR DO NEXT VISIT

ACTIVITY & RATING

_____	☆ ☆ ☆ ☆ ☆	_____	☆ ☆ ☆ ☆ ☆
_____	☆ ☆ ☆ ☆ ☆	_____	☆ ☆ ☆ ☆ ☆
_____	☆ ☆ ☆ ☆ ☆	_____	☆ ☆ ☆ ☆ ☆
_____	☆ ☆ ☆ ☆ ☆	_____	☆ ☆ ☆ ☆ ☆
_____	☆ ☆ ☆ ☆ ☆	_____	☆ ☆ ☆ ☆ ☆
_____	☆ ☆ ☆ ☆ ☆	_____	☆ ☆ ☆ ☆ ☆
_____	☆ ☆ ☆ ☆ ☆	_____	☆ ☆ ☆ ☆ ☆
	☆ ☆ ☆ ☆ ☆		☆ ☆ ☆ ☆ ☆

TRIP MEMORIES & OTHER NOTES:

NATIONAL PARK TRIP PLANNER:

City: **State:**

Anticipated Weather:

Trip Start/End Date:_____

ACCOMMODATIONS: _____

PHONE: _____ PARK CELL RECEPTION ☐

PETS ALLOWED: ☐ PARK WIFI: ☐

SUPPLIES:

PARK FEES

PARK ENTRANCE: _____

LODGING PER NIGHT: _____

VEHICLE REGISTRATION: _____

OTHER FEES: _____

_____

_____

TO DO:

☐ LODGING RESERVATIONS

☐ PARK ENTRANCE PASS

☐ NATIONAL PARK/FED LANDS PASS

☐ TRIP PLAN FOR EMERGENCY
CONTACT

☐ SAFETY LEADER: _____

☐ VEHICLE REGISTERED, IF
REQUIRED

☐ DOWNLOAD NATIONAL PARK APP

☐ SAVED PARK FOR OFFLINE USE

☐ PACKED THE 10 ESSENTIALS

☐

☐

☐

ACTIVITY & PLACES TO VISIT ITINERARY

DATE/TIME	ACTIVITY	RESERVATIONS

OTHER NOTES:

NATIONAL PARK:

Overall Rating ☆ ☆ ☆ ☆ ☆

FAVORITE ACTIVITY:_____

FAVORITE TRAIL:_____

TOP WILDLIFE SIGHTS:_____

BEST SCENIC VIEWS_____

ACTIVITY ☆ ☆ ☆ ☆ ☆

LODGING ☆ ☆ ☆ ☆ ☆

FLORA & FAUNA ☆ ☆ ☆ ☆ ☆

CROWDS ☆ ☆ ☆ ☆ ☆

STARGAZING ☆ ☆ ☆ ☆ ☆

PASSPORT STAMP & MEMORABILIA

TO REMEMBER OR DO NEXT VISIT

ACTIVITY & RATING

_____	☆ ☆ ☆ ☆ ☆	_____	☆ ☆ ☆ ☆ ☆
_____	☆ ☆ ☆ ☆ ☆	_____	☆ ☆ ☆ ☆ ☆
_____	☆ ☆ ☆ ☆ ☆	_____	☆ ☆ ☆ ☆ ☆
_____	☆ ☆ ☆ ☆ ☆	_____	☆ ☆ ☆ ☆ ☆
_____	☆ ☆ ☆ ☆ ☆	_____	☆ ☆ ☆ ☆ ☆
_____	☆ ☆ ☆ ☆ ☆	_____	☆ ☆ ☆ ☆ ☆
_____	☆ ☆ ☆ ☆ ☆	_____	☆ ☆ ☆ ☆ ☆
_____	☆ ☆ ☆ ☆ ☆	_____	☆ ☆ ☆ ☆ ☆

TRIP MEMORIES & OTHER NOTES:

NATIONAL PARK TRIP PLANNER:

City: **State:**

Trip Start/End Date:_____

Anticipated Weather:

ACCOMMODATIONS: _____

PHONE: _____ PARK CELL RECEPTION ☐

PETS ALLOWED: ☐ PARK WIFI: ☐

SUPPLIES:

PARK FEES

PARK ENTRANCE:_____

LODGING PER NIGHT:_____

VEHICLE REGISTRATION: _____

OTHER FEES:_____

_____

_____

TO DO:

☐ LODGING RESERVATIONS
☐ PARK ENTRANCE PASS
☐ NATIONAL PARK/FED LANDS PASS
☐ TRIP PLAN FOR EMERGENCY CONTACT
☐ SAFETY LEADER: _____
☐ VEHICLE REGISTERED, IF REQUIRED
☐ DOWNLOAD NATIONAL PARK APP
☐ SAVED PARK FOR OFFLINE USE
☐ PACKED THE 10 ESSENTIALS
☐
☐
☐

ACTIVITY & PLACES TO VISIT ITINERARY

DATE/TIME	ACTIVITY	RESERVATIONS

OTHER NOTES:

NATIONAL PARK:

Overall Rating ☆ ☆ ☆ ☆ ☆

FAVORITE ACTIVITY:_____

FAVORITE TRAIL:_____

TOP WILDLIFE SIGHTS:_____

BEST SCENIC VIEWS_____

ACTIVITY ☆ ☆ ☆ ☆ ☆

LODGING ☆ ☆ ☆ ☆ ☆

FLORA & FAUNA ☆ ☆ ☆ ☆ ☆

CROWDS ☆ ☆ ☆ ☆ ☆

STARGAZING ☆ ☆ ☆ ☆ ☆

PASSPORT STAMP & MEMORABILIA

TO REMEMBER OR DO NEXT VISIT

ACTIVITY & RATING

_____	☆ ☆ ☆ ☆ ☆	_____	☆ ☆ ☆ ☆ ☆
_____	☆ ☆ ☆ ☆ ☆	_____	☆ ☆ ☆ ☆ ☆
_____	☆ ☆ ☆ ☆ ☆	_____	☆ ☆ ☆ ☆ ☆
_____	☆ ☆ ☆ ☆ ☆	_____	☆ ☆ ☆ ☆ ☆
_____	☆ ☆ ☆ ☆ ☆	_____	☆ ☆ ☆ ☆ ☆
_____	☆ ☆ ☆ ☆ ☆	_____	☆ ☆ ☆ ☆ ☆
_____	☆ ☆ ☆ ☆ ☆	_____	☆ ☆ ☆ ☆ ☆
_____	☆ ☆ ☆ ☆ ☆	_____	☆ ☆ ☆ ☆ ☆

TRIP MEMORIES & OTHER NOTES:

National Park Trip Planner:

City: **State:**

Trip Start/End Date:_____

Anticipated Weather:

ACCOMMODATIONS: _____

PHONE: _____   PARK CELL RECEPTION ☐

PETS ALLOWED: ☐   PARK WIFI: ☐

SUPPLIES:

TO DO:

☐ LODGING RESERVATIONS
☐ PARK ENTRANCE PASS
☐ NATIONAL PARK/FED LANDS PASS
☐ TRIP PLAN FOR EMERGENCY
   CONTACT
☐ SAFETY LEADER: _____
☐ VEHICLE REGISTERED, IF
   REQUIRED
☐ DOWNLOAD NATIONAL PARK APP
☐ SAVED PARK FOR OFFLINE USE
☐ PACKED THE 10 ESSENTIALS
☐
☐
☐

PARK FEES

PARK ENTRANCE:_____

LODGING PER NIGHT:_____

VEHICLE REGISTRATION: _____

OTHER FEES:_____

_____

_____

ACTIVITY & PLACES TO VISIT ITINERARY

DATE/TIME	ACTIVITY	RESERVATIONS

OTHER NOTES:

NATIONAL PARK:

Overall Rating ☆ ☆ ☆ ☆ ☆

FAVORITE ACTIVITY:_____

FAVORITE TRAIL:_____

TOP WILDLIFE SIGHTS:_____

BEST SCENIC VIEWS_____

ACTIVITY ☆ ☆ ☆ ☆ ☆

LODGING ☆ ☆ ☆ ☆ ☆

FLORA & FAUNA ☆ ☆ ☆ ☆ ☆

CROWDS ☆ ☆ ☆ ☆ ☆

STARGAZING ☆ ☆ ☆ ☆ ☆

PASSPORT STAMP & MEMORABILIA

TO REMEMBER OR DO NEXT VISIT

ACTIVITY & RATING

_____	☆ ☆ ☆ ☆ ☆	_____	☆ ☆ ☆ ☆ ☆
_____	☆ ☆ ☆ ☆ ☆	_____	☆ ☆ ☆ ☆ ☆
_____	☆ ☆ ☆ ☆ ☆	_____	☆ ☆ ☆ ☆ ☆
_____	☆ ☆ ☆ ☆ ☆	_____	☆ ☆ ☆ ☆ ☆
_____	☆ ☆ ☆ ☆ ☆	_____	☆ ☆ ☆ ☆ ☆
_____	☆ ☆ ☆ ☆ ☆	_____	☆ ☆ ☆ ☆ ☆
_____	☆ ☆ ☆ ☆ ☆	_____	☆ ☆ ☆ ☆ ☆
	☆ ☆ ☆ ☆ ☆		☆ ☆ ☆ ☆ ☆

TRIP MEMORIES & OTHER NOTES:

NATIONAL PARK TRIP PLANNER:

City: _____ **State:** _____ **Anticipated Weather:**

Trip Start/End Date: _____

ACCOMMODATIONS: _____

PHONE: _____ PARK CELL RECEPTION ☐

PETS ALLOWED: ☐ PARK WIFI: ☐

SUPPLIES:

TO DO:

- ☐ LODGING RESERVATIONS
- ☐ PARK ENTRANCE PASS
- ☐ NATIONAL PARK/FED LANDS PASS
- ☐ TRIP PLAN FOR EMERGENCY CONTACT
- ☐ SAFETY LEADER: _____
- ☐ VEHICLE REGISTERED, IF REQUIRED
- ☐ DOWNLOAD NATIONAL PARK APP
- ☐ SAVED PARK FOR OFFLINE USE
- ☐ PACKED THE 10 ESSENTIALS
- ☐
- ☐
- ☐

PARK FEES

PARK ENTRANCE: _____

LODGING PER NIGHT: _____

VEHICLE REGISTRATION: _____

OTHER FEES: _____

_____

_____

ACTIVITY & PLACES TO VISIT ITINERARY

DATE/TIME	ACTIVITY	RESERVATIONS

OTHER NOTES:

NATIONAL PARK:

Overall Rating ☆ ☆ ☆ ☆ ☆

FAVORITE ACTIVITY:_____

FAVORITE TRAIL:_____

TOP WILDLIFE SIGHTS:_____

BEST SCENIC VIEWS_____

ACTIVITY ☆ ☆ ☆ ☆ ☆

LODGING ☆ ☆ ☆ ☆ ☆

FLORA & FAUNA ☆ ☆ ☆ ☆ ☆

CROWDS ☆ ☆ ☆ ☆ ☆

STARGAZING ☆ ☆ ☆ ☆ ☆

PASSPORT STAMP & MEMORABILIA

TO REMEMBER OR DO NEXT VISIT

ACTIVITY & RATING

_____	☆ ☆ ☆ ☆ ☆	_____	☆ ☆ ☆ ☆ ☆
_____	☆ ☆ ☆ ☆ ☆	_____	☆ ☆ ☆ ☆ ☆
_____	☆ ☆ ☆ ☆ ☆	_____	☆ ☆ ☆ ☆ ☆
_____	☆ ☆ ☆ ☆ ☆	_____	☆ ☆ ☆ ☆ ☆
_____	☆ ☆ ☆ ☆ ☆	_____	☆ ☆ ☆ ☆ ☆
_____	☆ ☆ ☆ ☆ ☆	_____	☆ ☆ ☆ ☆ ☆
_____	☆ ☆ ☆ ☆ ☆	_____	☆ ☆ ☆ ☆ ☆
_____	☆ ☆ ☆ ☆ ☆	_____	☆ ☆ ☆ ☆ ☆

TRIP MEMORIES & OTHER NOTES:

NATIONAL PARK TRIP PLANNER:

City: **State:**

Trip Start/End Date: _____

Anticipated Weather:

ACCOMMODATIONS: _____

PHONE: _____   PARK CELL RECEPTION ☐

PETS ALLOWED: ☐   PARK WIFI: ☐

SUPPLIES:

PARK FEES

PARK ENTRANCE: _____

LODGING PER NIGHT: _____

VEHICLE REGISTRATION: _____

OTHER FEES: _____

_____

_____

TO DO:

☐ LODGING RESERVATIONS

☐ PARK ENTRANCE PASS

☐ NATIONAL PARK/FED LANDS PASS

☐ TRIP PLAN FOR EMERGENCY
   CONTACT

☐ SAFETY LEADER: _____

☐ VEHICLE REGISTERED, IF
   REQUIRED

☐ DOWNLOAD NATIONAL PARK APP

☐ SAVED PARK FOR OFFLINE USE

☐ PACKED THE 10 ESSENTIALS

☐

☐

☐

ACTIVITY & PLACES TO VISIT ITINERARY

DATE/TIME	ACTIVITY	RESERVATIONS

OTHER NOTES:

NATIONAL PARK:

Overall Rating ☆ ☆ ☆ ☆ ☆

FAVORITE ACTIVITY:_____

FAVORITE TRAIL:_____

TOP WILDLIFE SIGHTS:_____

BEST SCENIC VIEWS_____

ACTIVITY ☆ ☆ ☆ ☆ ☆

LODGING ☆ ☆ ☆ ☆ ☆

FLORA & FAUNA ☆ ☆ ☆ ☆ ☆

CROWDS ☆ ☆ ☆ ☆ ☆

STARGAZING ☆ ☆ ☆ ☆ ☆

PASSPORT STAMP & MEMORABILIA

TO REMEMBER OR DO NEXT VISIT

ACTIVITY & RATING

_____	☆ ☆ ☆ ☆ ☆	_____	☆ ☆ ☆ ☆ ☆
_____	☆ ☆ ☆ ☆ ☆	_____	☆ ☆ ☆ ☆ ☆
_____	☆ ☆ ☆ ☆ ☆	_____	☆ ☆ ☆ ☆ ☆
_____	☆ ☆ ☆ ☆ ☆	_____	☆ ☆ ☆ ☆ ☆
_____	☆ ☆ ☆ ☆ ☆	_____	☆ ☆ ☆ ☆ ☆
_____	☆ ☆ ☆ ☆ ☆	_____	☆ ☆ ☆ ☆ ☆
_____	☆ ☆ ☆ ☆ ☆	_____	☆ ☆ ☆ ☆ ☆
	☆ ☆ ☆ ☆ ☆		☆ ☆ ☆ ☆ ☆

TRIP MEMORIES & OTHER NOTES:

Trail Blazing Logbook

Trail Name	Date	Park	Method	Miles and Duration	Rating
					☆ ☆ ☆ ☆ ☆
					☆ ☆ ☆ ☆ ☆
					☆ ☆ ☆ ☆ ☆
					☆ ☆ ☆ ☆ ☆
					☆ ☆ ☆ ☆ ☆
					☆ ☆ ☆ ☆ ☆
					☆ ☆ ☆ ☆ ☆
					☆ ☆ ☆ ☆ ☆
					☆ ☆ ☆ ☆ ☆
					☆ ☆ ☆ ☆ ☆
					☆ ☆ ☆ ☆ ☆
					☆ ☆ ☆ ☆ ☆
					☆ ☆ ☆ ☆ ☆
					☆ ☆ ☆ ☆ ☆
					☆ ☆ ☆ ☆ ☆
					☆ ☆ ☆ ☆ ☆

Trail Blazing Logbook

Trail Name Date Park	Method	Miles and Duration	Rating
			☆ ☆ ☆ ☆ ☆
			☆ ☆ ☆ ☆ ☆
			☆ ☆ ☆ ☆ ☆
			☆ ☆ ☆ ☆ ☆
			☆ ☆ ☆ ☆ ☆
			☆ ☆ ☆ ☆ ☆
			☆ ☆ ☆ ☆ ☆
			☆ ☆ ☆ ☆ ☆
			☆ ☆ ☆ ☆ ☆
			☆ ☆ ☆ ☆ ☆
			☆ ☆ ☆ ☆ ☆
			☆ ☆ ☆ ☆ ☆
			☆ ☆ ☆ ☆ ☆
			☆ ☆ ☆ ☆ ☆
			☆ ☆ ☆ ☆ ☆
			☆ ☆ ☆ ☆ ☆

Trail Blazing Logbook

Trail Name	Date	Park	Method	Miles and Duration	Rating
					☆☆☆ ☆☆
					☆☆☆ ☆☆
					☆☆☆ ☆☆
					☆☆☆ ☆☆
					☆☆☆ ☆☆
					☆☆☆ ☆☆
					☆☆☆ ☆☆
					☆☆☆ ☆☆
					☆☆☆ ☆☆
					☆☆☆ ☆☆
					☆☆☆ ☆☆
					☆☆☆ ☆☆
					☆☆☆ ☆☆
					☆☆☆ ☆☆
					☆☆☆ ☆☆
					☆☆☆ ☆☆

Trail Blazing Logbook

Trail Name Date Park	Method	Miles and Duration	Rating
			☆☆☆ ☆☆
			☆☆☆ ☆☆
			☆☆☆ ☆☆
			☆☆☆ ☆☆
			☆☆☆ ☆☆
			☆☆☆ ☆☆
			☆☆☆ ☆☆
			☆☆☆ ☆☆
			☆☆☆ ☆☆
			☆☆☆ ☆☆
			☆☆☆ ☆☆
			☆☆☆ ☆☆
			☆☆☆ ☆☆
			☆☆☆ ☆☆
			☆☆☆ ☆☆
			☆☆☆ ☆☆

Trail Blazing Logbook

Trail Name	Date	Park	Method	Miles and Duration	Rating
					☆☆☆ ☆☆
					☆☆☆ ☆☆
					☆☆☆ ☆☆
					☆☆☆ ☆☆
					☆☆☆ ☆☆
					☆☆☆ ☆☆
					☆☆☆ ☆☆
					☆☆☆ ☆☆
					☆☆☆ ☆☆
					☆☆☆ ☆☆
					☆☆☆ ☆☆
					☆☆☆ ☆☆
					☆☆☆ ☆☆
					☆☆☆ ☆☆
					☆☆☆ ☆☆
					☆☆☆ ☆☆

Trail Blazing Logbook

Trail Name Date Park	Method	Miles and Duration	Rating
			☆☆☆ ☆☆
			☆☆☆ ☆☆
			☆☆☆ ☆☆
			☆☆☆ ☆☆
			☆☆☆ ☆☆
			☆☆☆ ☆☆
			☆☆☆ ☆☆
			☆☆☆ ☆☆
			☆☆☆ ☆☆
			☆☆☆ ☆☆
			☆☆☆ ☆☆
			☆☆☆ ☆☆
			☆☆☆ ☆☆
			☆☆☆ ☆☆
			☆☆☆ ☆☆
			☆☆☆ ☆☆

Flora & Fauna at-a-glance

Location of Sighting (Date and Park)	Category	Scientific / Common Name

Flora & Fauna at-a-glance

Location of Sighting (Date and Park)	Category	Scientific / Common Name

Flora & Fauna at-a-glance

Location of Sighting (Date and Park)	Category	Scientific / Common Name

Flora & Fauna at-a-glance

Location of Sighting (Date and Park)	Category	Scientific / Common Name

Flora and Fauna Notes

Flora and Fauna Notes

Birdwatching Tally

Location of Sighting (Date and Park)	Bird Name	Tally

Birdwatching Tally

Location of Sighting	Bird Name	Tally
(Date and Park)		

Birdwatching Tally

Location of Sighting (Date and Park)	Bird Name	Tally

Birdwatching Tally

Location of Sighting	Bird Name	Tally
(Date and Park)		

BirdWatching Notes

BirdWatching Notes

Scan-n-See

Check out park information using these interactive QR codes with any wireless connected digital camera. Click your camera icon on your device and place in front of any QR code below. When the frame appears around the park you are wanting to see, click or touch inside the frame and the scan will take you to the webpage for that park. You can check on the most recent information about the park and make your plans accordingly.

Indiana Dunes

Isle Royale

Joshua Tree

Katmai

Kenai Fjords

Kings Canyon

Kobuk Valley

Lake Clark

Lassen Volcanic

Mammoth Cave

Mesa Verde

Mount Rainier

New River Gorge

North Cascades

Olympic

PetrifiedForest

Pinnacles

Redwood

Rocky Mountains

Saguaro

Sequoia

Shenandoah

Theo Roosevelt

Virgin Islands

Voyageurs

White Sands

Wind Cave

Wrangell-Elias

Yellowstone

Yosemite

Zion

ACADIA
25 Visitor Center Road
Hulls Cove Visitor Center
Bar Harbor, ME 04609
207-288-3338

AMERICAN SAMOA
Pago Pago, AS 96799

684-633-7082 X22

ARCHES
N Hwy 191, Moab,
84532, UT

435-719-2299

BADLANDS
25216 Ben Reifel Road
Interior, SD 57750

605-433-5361

BIG BEND
1 Panther Junction
Big Bend National Park,
TX 79834
432-477-2251

BISCAYNE
9700 SW 328th Street
Sir Lancelot Jones Way
Homestead, FL 33033
305-230-1144

BLACK CANYON OF THE GUNNISON
South Rim Visitor Center
9800 Highway 347
Montrose, CO 81401
970-641-2337 X205

BRYCE CANYON
Highway 63
Bryce Canyon National Park
Bryce, UT 84764
435-834-5322

CANYONLANDS
2282 Resource Blvd.
Moab , UT 84532

435-719-2313

CAPITOL REEF
52 West Headquarters Drive
Torrey, UT 84775

435-425-3791
CARE_INFORMATION@NPS.GOV

CARLSBAD CAVERNS
727 Carlsbad Caverns Highway
Carlsbad, NM 88220

575-785-2232

CHANNEL ISLANDS
1901 Spinnaker Drive
Ventura, CA 93001

805-658-5730

CONGAREE
100 National Park Road
Hopkins, SC 29061

803-776-4396

CRATER LAKE
Crater Lake , OR 97604

541-594-3000

CUYAHOGA VALLEY
6947 Riverview Road
Peninsula, OH 44264

440-717-3890

DEATH VALLEY
California Hwy 190
U.S. Route 95 Nevada

760-786-3200

DENALI
Mile 237 Highway 3
Denali Park, AK 99755

907-683-9532

DRY TORTUGAS
40001 SR-9336
Homestead, FL 33034

305-242-7700

EVERGLADES
40001 State Road-9336
Homestead, FL 33034
        305-242-7700

GREAT SMOKY MOUNTAINS
Sugarlands Visitor Center
1420 Little River Road
Gatlinburg, TN 37738
        305-242-7700

GATES OF THE ARCTIC
101 Dunkel St
Fairbanks, AK 99701

        907-459-3730

GUADALUPE MOUNTAINS
400 Pine Canyon
Salt Flat, TX 79847

        915-828-3251

GATEWAY ARCH
Fourth Street between
Market and Chestnut streets
St. Louis, MO 63102
        314-655-1600

HALEAKALA
Haleakala National Park
Makawao , HI 96768
        808-572-4400

GLACIER
64 Grinnell Drive
 Park Headquarters
West Glacier, MT 59936
        406-888-7800

HAWAII VOLCANOES
1 Crater Rim Drive
Hawaii National Park, HI 96718

        808-985-6011

GLACIER BAY
1 Park Road
Gustavus, AK 99826

        907-697-2230

HOT SPRINGS
Fordyce Bathhouse Visitor Cntr
369 Central Avenue
Hot Springs, AR 71901
        501-620-6715

GRAND CANYON
20 South Entrance Road
Grand Canyon, AZ 86023

        928-638-7888

INDIANA DUNES
1215 SR-49
Porter, IN 46304

        219-395-1882

GRAND TETON
103 Headquarters Loop
Moose, WY 83012

        307-739-3399

ISLE ROYALE
Mainland Headquarters
800 East Lakeshore Drive
Houghton, MI 49931
        906-482-0984

GREAT BASIN
Lehman Caves Visitor Center
Nevada 488
Baker, NV 89311
        775-234-7331

JOSHUA TREE
74485 National Park Drive
Twentynine Palms,
CA 92277-3597
        760-367-5500

GREAT SAND DUNES
Visitor Center
11999 State Highway 150
Mosca, CO 81146
        719-378-6395

KATMAI
1000 Silver Street
Building 603
King Salmon, AK 99613
        907-246-3305

KENAI FJORDA
Main Park Visitor Center
Seward Small Boat Harbor
Seward , AK 99664
907-422-0500

NORTH CASCADES
810 State Route 20
Sedro-Woolley, WA 98284

360-854-7200

KINGS CANYON
47050 Generals Highway
Three Rivers, CA 93271

559-565-3341

OLYMPIC
Olympic National Park Visitor Cntr
3002 Mount Angeles Road
Port Angeles , WA 98362
360-565-3130

KOBUK VALLEY
171 3rd Ave
Kotzebue, AK 99752

907-442-3890

PETRIFIED FOREST
1 Park Road
Petrified Forest, AZ 86028

928-524-6228

LAKE CLARK
Alaska Peninsula
Not located on road system
Port Alsworth, AK 99653
907-644-3626

PINNACLES
5000 East Entrance Road
Paicines, CA 95043

831-389-4486

LASSEN VOLCANIC
38050 Highway 36 East
Park Headquarters
Mineral, CA 96063
530-595-4480

REDWOOD
1111 Second Street
Crescent City, CA 95531

707-464-6101

MAMMOTH CAVES
1 Visitor Center Parkway
Mammoth Cave, KY
42259-0007
270-758-2180

ROCKY MOUNTAIN
1000 US Hwy 36
Estes Park, CO 80517

970-586-1206

MESA VERDE
Mile .7 Headquarters Loop Road
Mesa Verde National Park,
CO 81330
970-529-4465

SAGUARO
3693 S Old Spanish Trail
Tucson , AZ 85730

520-733-5153

MOUNT RAINIER
39000 State Route 706 E,
Ashford, WA 98304

360-569-2211

SEQUOIA
47050 Generals Highway
Three Rivers, CA 93271

559-565-3341

NEW RIVER GORGE
104 Main Street
Glen Jean, WV 25846

304-465-0508

SHENANDOAH
3655 US Hwy. 211 East Luray,
VA 22835-9036

540-999-3500

THEODORE ROOSEVELT
315 Second Avenue
Medora, ND 58645

701-623-4466

VIRGIN ISLANDS
1300 Cruz Bay Creek
St. John, VI 00830

340-776-6201 X238

VOYAGEURS
Voyageurs National Park HQ
360 Hwy 11 East
International Falls, MN 56649
218-283-6600

WHITE SANDS
19955 Highway 70 West
Alamogordo, NM 88310

575-479-6124

WIND CAVE
26611 US Highway 385
Hot Springs, SD 57747

605-745-4600

WRANGELL--ST ELIAS
Mile 106.8 Richardson Highway
Copper Center , AK 99573

907-822-5234

YELLOWSTONE
2 Officers Row
Yellowstone National Park HQ
Yellowstone National Park,
WY 82190   307-344-7381

YOSEMITE
Tioga Rd Hwy 120 & Hwy 140
Yosemite National Park,
CA 95389

209-372-0200

ZION
1 Zion Park Blvd.
State Route 9
Springdale, UT 84767

435-772-3256

Park	Date	Location	Area
Yellowstone	March 1, 1872	Wyoming, Montana, Idaho	2,219,790.71

Yellowstone National Park is home to many geothermal features, including springs with vivid colors and hot mud pots. The park features many geysers, the best known of which is Old Faithful. The Grand Canyon of the Yellowstone River has several waterfalls and four mountain ranges. This is one of the best places in the US to see wildlife. It has wolves, grizzly bears, black bears, lynxes, bison, and elk.

Sequoia	September 25,1890	California	404,062.63

This park protects Giant Forest, which has trees that are among the largest in the world. This includes the General Sherman, the largest measured tree in the park. There are also over 240 caves and a long stretch of Sierra Nevada mountains where you'll find some of the tallest mountains in the contiguous US and a large granite dome, Moro Rock.

Yosemite	October 1, 1890	California	761,747.50

Yosemite is a national park in California with cliffs, tall waterfalls, and old-growth forests. Half Dome and El Capitan loom above the park's centerpiece, Yosemite Valley. One of the North America's tallest waterfalls, Yosemite Falls, drops 739 meters from its sheer vertical walls. Three giant sequoia groves live in the mountains that are covered in ice. A wide variety of rare plant and animal species make their home here.

Mount Ranier	March 2, 1899	Washington	36,381.64

Mount Rainier National Park is known for its active stratovolcano, which is covered with 26 named glaciers. The longest and largest of these glaciers are Carbon Glacier and Emmons Glacier. In the park, visitors can enjoy many activities, such as hiking. More than half of Mount Rainer National Park is covered by snow and ice. The Longmire visitor center is the start of the Wonderland Trail, which encircles the mountain.

Crater Lake	May 22, 1902	Oregon	183,224.05

Crater Lake is in the caldera of an ancient volcano that collapsed 7,700 years ago. It is the deepest lake in the United States and is known for its vivid blue color and water clarity. Wizard Island and the Phantom Ship are the newer volcanic formations within the caldera. As there are no inlets or outlets, it is continuously replenished only by rain.

Wind Cave	January 9, 1903	South Dakota	33,970.84

Wind Cave is home to a calcite formation, needle-like growths and a wind that's created as the air changes pressure. This cave is one of the longest in the world. Above ground, there is a mixed-grass prairie with animals such as bison, black-footed ferrets, and prairie dogs. Underground is a cave. It is culturally significant to the Lakota people as it is seen as the spot where they were created (presumably by some deity).

Mesa Verde	June 29, 1906	Colorado	52,485.17

This is an area with around 4,000 archaeological sites of people who lived here for at least 700 years. Balcony House is one of many cliff dwellings built in the 12th and 13th centuries. They include Cliff Palace, with 150 rooms, and are one of the earliest examples of urban planning in North America.

Glacier	May 11, 1910	Montana	1,013,125.99

The USPA side of the Waterton-Glacier International Peace Park is made of 26 glaciers, 130 lakes, and Rocky Mountains. There are historic hotels and the famous Going-to-the-Sun Road in this region. The local mountains were formed by an overthrust and are rich with fossils from the Paleozoic era. This park also contains Triple Divide Peak, which forms the boundary between three water basins: the Atlantic, Pacific, and Arctic oceans.

| Rocky Mountain | January 26, 1915 | Colorado | 265,807.25 |

This area is bisected by the Continental Divide and has ecosystems that vary from riparian lakes to montane and subalpine forests to treeless alpine tundra. Wildlife including mule deer, bighorn sheep, black bears, and cougars inhabit its igneous mountains and glacial valleys. Longs Peak is a popular Colorado fourteener that is also scenic and close to Bear Lake. The road up Longs peaks is called Trail Ridge Road, and it reaches an elevation of 12,000 feet.

| Hawaii Volcanoes | August 1, 1916 | Hawaii | 325,605.28 |

This park in Hawaii protects the Kilauea and Mauna Loa volcanoes, two of the world's most active geological features. The park's diverse ecosystems range from tropical forests at sea level to dry lava beds which are more than 13,000 feet (4000 meters) high.

| Lassen Volcanic | August 9, 1916 | California | 106,589.02 |

Lassen Peak is the largest lava dome volcano in the world and is also joined by all three other types of volcanoes: shield, cinder cone, and composite. Though Lassen Peak has not erupted in decades, most of the rest of the park is continuously active. There are hydrothermal features including fumaroles, boiling pools, and bubbling mud pots due to molten rock beneath the peak.

| Denali | February 26, 1917 | Alaska | 4,740,911.16 |

the Alaska Range's tallest and highest point, is serviced by a single park to Wonder Lake. The crest of the Denali range is covered with glaciers and boreal forest. Wildlife includes grizzly bears, Dall sheep, Porcupine caribou, and wolves.

| Acadia | February 26, 1919 | Maine | 49,076.63 |

This national park covers most of Mount Desert Island and other coastal islands. The tallest mountain on the Atlantic coast of the United States, granite peaks, ocean shoreline, woodlands, and lakes can be found here. Freshwater & estuary areas are present as well as forest & intertidal zones.

| Grand Canyon | February 26, 1919 | Arizona | 1,201,647.03 |

The Grand Canyon is 277 miles (446 km) long and can be up to 1 mile (1.6 km) deep and up to 15 miles (24 km) wide. The Colorado Plateau comprises multicolored layers that have been exposed over the course of millions of years because of erosion. These layers can be seen from trails on both north and south rim.

| Zion | November 19, 1919 | Utah | 147,242.66 |

Zion National Park is a beautiful and deep landscape that includes mesas, towers, and Canyons. These sandstone features are among many there that include Virign River Narrows. The Virgin River has formed four ecosystems with different climates, desert, riparian, woodland, and coniferous forest.

| Hot Springs | March 4, 1921 | Arkansas | 5,554.15 |

Hot Springs National Park was first established as a federal reserve by Congress on April 20, 1832. The park is an opportunity to relax in a historic location with natural hot springs flowing from the Ouachita Mountains. Bathhouse Row in Hot Springs is made up of examples of 19th-century architecture. It's one of the first national parks and also the smallest. The designation was updated in 2018

Bryce Canyon	February 25, 1928	Utah	35,835.08

Bryce Canyon is a geological amphitheater located on the Paunsaugunt Plateau with hundreds of hoodoos of different colors. Ancient inhabitants, like Native Americans and Mormon pioneers, once settled around this region.

Grand Teton	February 26, 1929	Wyoming	310,044.36

Grand Teton is the tallest mountain in the Teton Range and is a site of incredible natural beauty. The Jackson Hole & its beautiful lakes living alongside craggy mountains provide a stunning backdrop to wildlife that live in this valley.

Carlsbad Caverns	May 14, 1930	New Mexico	46,766.45

The Carlsbad Caverns are home to over 400,000 Mexican free-tailed bats and eleven other species. Carlsbad also has 118 caves, the longest of them being 120 miles long. The Big Room is notable for its size, with an area of 10 acres (8 hectares), and is over 4,000 feet long.

Everglades	May 30, 1934	Florida	1,508,938.57

The Everglades in the US is a large and diverse wildlife environment. For many years, some areas have been drained for development, which has led to destruction of the environment. Restoration projects aim to restore wildlife by removing buildings & reclaiming drainage canals.

Great Smoky Mountains	June 15, 1934	North Carolina, Tennessee	522,426.88

The Great Smoky Mountain in the Appalachian Mountains is home to over 400 vertebrate species, 100 tree species, and 5000 plant species. Hiking is the park's main attraction. The park has over 800 miles of trails, including 70 miles of the Appalachian Trail. Other activities include fishing, horseback riding, and touring nearly 80 historic structures.

Shenandoah	December 26, 1935	Virginia	199,223.77

Shenandoah forest covers the Blue Ridge Mountains and is covered densely with hardwood. The Skyline Drive and Appalachian Trail run the entire length of this park and over 500 miles of hiking trails that pass by many scenic landmarks.

Olympic	June 29, 1938	Washington	922,649.41

Olympic National Park is a 2,400 square mile area on the Pacific coast. Bordering the Quinault Indian Nation and filled with a variety of unique landscapes. This park has several climates including rainforests and mountainous areas. The Hoh Rainforest receives an average of 126 inches per year, while Quinault gets about 160 inches per year.

Kings Canyon	March 4, 1940	California	461,901.20

Kings River is home to several sequoia groves and the 2nd largest tree in the world. This park also features sculptor Kings River, part of the San Joaquin River, and Boyden Cave.Though Kings Canyon National Park is classified as such, it subsumes General Grand National Park, which had been established on October 1, 1890 as the United States' 4th national park.

Isle Royale	April 3, 1940	Michigan	571,790.30

Isle Royale is the largest island in Lake Superior, and despite its small size (only 69 square miles), it has over 400 smaller islands and over 100 different types of bird species. Wolves threaten moose populations, but this relationship may be changing because the numbers of moose are thriving.

MammothCave	July 1, 1941	Kentucky	54,011.91

Mammoth Cave is one of the world's longest cave systems and contains a myriad of bat species, elusive cave shrimp, and obscure aquatic creatures. It provides plenty of recreational opportunities on the Green River, which has a 70-mile hiking trail system.

Big Bend	June 12, 1944	Texas	801,163.21

The Rio Grande defines the park, and the park is a significant destination for backcountry recreation in arid Chisos Mountains and canyons along the Rio Grande. Fossils and artifacts of Cretaceous & Tertiary animals and of Native Americans are found within the state.

Virgin Islands	August 2, 1956	U.S. Virgin Islands	15,052.53

This national park on the U.S.-flagged island of Saint John has preserved its beaches, mangrove forests, seagrass beds, and coral reefs. There are also Taíno archaeological sites here that date back to Columbus's time in which you can explore. These features are accompanied by the ruins of sugar plantations from decades ago.

Haleakala	July 1, 1961	Hawaii	33,264.62

The Haleakala Volcano on Maui has a large crater with many cinder cones, Hosmer's Grove of alien trees, the Kipahulu section's pools of freshwater fish, and native Hawaiian geese. The park protects the most ancient living things—the plants-and all of their habitats.

PetrifiedForest	December 9, 1962	Arizona	221,390.21

The Chinle Formation has a considerable amount of 225-million-year-old petrified wood, along with red-colored volcanic rock called bentonite. Dinosaur fossils are also present, as well as 350 Native American sites for ceremonial purposes.

Canyonlands	September 12, 1964	Utah	337,597.83

The Canyonlands now is a maze of canyons, buttes, and mesas that were down with the combined effort of tributaries of the Colorado River & Green River. It has 3 districts. It also contains rock pinnacles & arches.

Guadalupe Mountains	October 15, 1966	Texas	86,367.10

The Guadalupe Peak park is enormous and boasts the highest point in Texas. The McKittrick Canyon, a corner of the arid Chihuahuan Desert, and a fossilized coral reef from the Permian era can all be found here.

North Cascades	October 2, 1968	Washington	504,780.94

The North Cascades Mountains can be found in Washington State. They are often mountainous and they are filled with ice. The geology is varied and complex, which allows visitors to explore many spots. The Stephen Mather Wilderness Area is home to four of the most popular hiking and climbing areas in the country: Cascade Pass, Mount Shuksan, Mount Triumph, and Eldorado Peak. There are 8 life zones here as well as 75 different mammal species and 1600 plant species. The Ross Lake National Recreation Area and Lake Chelan National Recreation Area both oversee parts of the wilderness.

Redwood	October 2, 1968	California	138,999.37

This park protects almost half of the remaining redwoods in California. There are three large river systems in the area, and 60 km of coast is protected. The prairie, estuary, coast, river, and forest ecosystems contain a wide variety of animal and plant species.

Arches
November 12, 1971 **Utah** 76,678.98

This site features more than 2000 natural sandstone arches, with some of the most popular being Delicate Arch, Landscape Arch and Double Arch. Millions of years of erosion in a desert climate have led to the formation of rocks and other geological features.

Capitol Reef
December 18, 1971 **Utah** 241,904.50

The park's waterpocket fold is a 100-mile monocline that exhibits the earth's diverse geologic layers. Other natural features include monoliths, cliffs, and sandstone domes like the United States Capitol.

Voyageurs
April 8, 1975 **Minnesota** 218,222.35

This park protecting four lakes near the Canada–US border is a site for canoeing, kayaking, and fishing. It also preserves a cultural history with Ojibwe Native Americans, French fur traders called voyageurs and gold miners. Formed by ancient glaciers, the region features tall bluffs, rock gardens, islands, bays and several historic buildings

Badlands
November 10, 1978 **South Dakota** 242,755.94

The badlands are an area of rugged terrain that includes buttes, spires, pinnacles and grassy mounds. The White River Badlands is an area of these badlands with the largest collection of late Eocene and Oligocene fossils in North America. The wildlife in this area includes bison, bighorn sheep and black-footed deer.

Theodore Roosevelt
November 10, 1978 **North Dakota** 70,446.89

The northern badlands region, which is part of Theodore Roosevelt National Park, was not only an intriguing place to visit but also influenced President Roosevelt. Roosevelt's cabin is the most famous attraction in the area. There are also scenic drives & hikes to take part in. Be sure to keep an eye out for animals like American bison, pronghorn, bighorn sheep, and wild horses!

Channel Islands
March 5, 1980 **California** 249,561.00

Five of the eight Channel Islands are protected with half of the park's area in water. The Channel Islands have been home to the Chumash people for a long time, and they have a Mediterranean ecosystem that is different from other parts of California. Here you can find over 2,000 species of land plants and animals. 145 are endemic to this island and it also has ferry services that can take you from the mainland.

Biscayne
June 28, 1980 **Florida** 172,971.11

The Florida Keys is an intriguing place worth visiting. The Biscayne Bay, central to the region, includes four distinct ecosystems: mangrove forests, the bay itself, the keys (some of which are offshore), and coral reefs. The following animals are threatened species: West Indian manatee, American crocodile, various sea turtles and the peregrine falcon.

Gates of the Arctic
December 2, 1980 **Alaska** 7,523,897.45

The northernmost national park in Alaska protects an expanse of pure wilderness and has no public facilities. It is home to the indigenous Alaskan tribes that have relied on this land & caribou for 11,000 years.

Glacier Bay
December 2, 1980 **Alaska** 3,223,383.43

Glacier Bay contains tidewater glaciers, mountains, fjords, and a temperate rainforest. It is also home to large populations of grizzly bears, mountain goats, whales, seals & eagles. Found in 1794 by George Vancouver the entire bay was covered by ice 100 years ago but has since receded over 65 miles.

Katmai | December 2, 1980 | Alaska | 3,674,529.33

This park on the Alaska Peninsula located near the Valley of Ten Thousand Smokes, an ash flow formed by the 1912 eruption of Novarupta, and Mount Katmai. It is home to over 2,000 grizzly bears that come here each year to catch spawning salmon. Other wildlife includes brown bears, wolves, lynx and beaver.

Kenai Fjords | December 2, 1980 | Alaska | 669,650.05

The Exit Glacier in Kenai, Alaska, is a popular tourist destination. The park that protects the icefield and fjords in which it lies, comprises a small accessible route, which leads to a viewing point near Seward. Boat tours offer views from further out across the area, and kayak tours from up close.

Kobuk Valley | December 2, 1980 | Alaska | 1,750,716.16

The Kobuk Valley protects 61 miles of the Kobuk River and three regions of sand dunes. The Great Kobuk, Little Kobuk, and Hunt River Sand Dunes can reach 100 feet high and 100 °F, making them some of the largest in Arctic. Twice a year, half a million caribou migrate through the dunes and across river bluffs that expose well preserved ice age fossils.

Lake Clark | December 2, 1980 | Alaska | 2,619,816.49

The region around Lake Clark features four active volcanoes, including Redoubt, as well as an abundance of rivers, glaciers, and waterfalls. Temperate rainforests, tundra plateau and three mountain ranges complete the landscape.

Wrangell–St. Elias | December 2, 1980 | Alaska | 8,323,146.48

The largest national park in the system protects the convergence of the Alaska, Chugach, Wrangell, and Saint Elias Ranges. The park has a lot of high mountains and volcanoes, including Mount Saint Elias. It's an incredible 1 million acres in size, 25% of it being glaciated, which you'll have access to.

Great Basin | October 27, 1986 | Nevada | 77,180.00

Wheeler Peak towers above Great Basin National Park, Nevada's second-tallest mountain. Home to 5,000-year-old Bristlecone Pines, a rock glacier, and the limestone Lehman Caves, the park's remote location makes it one of the country's darkest places to go stargazing. Wildlife in the American West includes the Townsend's big-eared bat, pronghorn, and Bonneville cutthroat trout.

American Samoa | October 31, 1988 | American Samoa | 8,256.67

The southernmost national park is on three Samoan islands and protects coral reefs, rainforests, volcanic mountains, and white beaches. The area is also home to flying foxes, brown boobies, sea turtles, and 900 species of fish.

Dry Tortugas | October 26, 1992 | Florida | 64,701.22

Fort Jefferson, a Civil War-era fort, is the largest masonry structure in the Western Hemisphere. It remains highly active during different seasons, which product habitats conducive to providing shelter for tens of thousands of shorebirds. Residents can often observe undisturbed coral reefs and shipwrecks around the Dry Tortugas Islands.

Saguaro	October 14, 1994	Arizona	92,867.42

This park is split into two districts, Rincon Mountain and Tucson Mountain. The dry Sonoran Desert here still maintains a diverse ecosystem that encompasses six different biomes. In the Sonoran Desert biome, one can find a wide variety of cacti and critters that have adapted to living in these harsh conditions. There's the famed giant saguaro, as well as barrel and cholla cacti, prickly pear plants, and a host of lesser-known animals such as long-nosed bats, spotted owls and javelinas.

Death Valley	October 31, 1994	California, Nevada	3,408,406.73

Death Valley is the hottest, lowest and driest place in the US. It has daytime temperatures that have exceeded 130 °F. Badwater Basin is an incredible place with one of the lowest points in North America. The park protects this unique environment but also areas like canyons, lava fields, sand dunes, mountains ranges and more. To top it all off, there are even springs & 1,000's of plant species to enjoy.

Joshua Tree	October 31, 1994	California	795,155.85

The Joshua Tree National Park is a beautiful, lush desert terrain. The park covers large areas of the Colorado and Mojave Deserts and the Little San Bernardino Mountains, populated by vast stands of Joshua trees. Large changes in elevation will lead you to the various environments including bleached sand dunes, dry lakes, rugged mountains, and maze-like clusters of monzogranite monoliths.

Black Canyon of the Gunnison	October 21, 1999	Colorado	30,779.83

The park protects one-quarter of the Gunnison River, which slices sheer canyon walls out of dark Precambrian-era rock. The canyon features some of the steepest cliffs and oldest rocks in North America, and is a popular site for rafting and climbing besides its many hiking trails. The canyon is a mixture of black gneiss and dark schist rock. It's a narrow gorge with steep walls, cool waterfalls, and crashing waves.

Cuyahoga Valley	October 11, 2000	Ohio	32,571.88

This park along the Cuyahoga River has all sorts of things to do, ranging from trails & waterfalls to historic houses. In the 1800s, people used mules to tow canal boats, which is why many people think this trail follows the canal.

Congaree	November 10, 2003	South Carolina	26,476.47

The Congaree National Park features the largest contiguous old-growth floodplain forest left in North America. There are some really tall trees here too! An elevated walkway called the Boardwalk Loop guides visitors through this 5,000 acre park.

Great Sand Dunes	September 24, 2004	Colorado	107,341.87

The tallest sand dunes in North America, up to 750 feet tall, were formed by deposits of the ancient Rio Grande in the San Luis Valley. Abutting a variety of grasslands, shrublands, and wetlands, the park also has alpine lakes, six 13,000-foot mountains, and old-growth forests.

Pinnacles	January 10, 2013	California	26,685.73

The park was named after the eroded remnants of a mountain that can be found there. The key feature are huge monoliths made of andesite & rhyolite. These are very popular destinations for rock climbers, while hikers can explore trails across the Coast Range wilderness. Pinnacles National Park is one of the few locations where you can see the

California condor in the wild. It also has a large population of prairie falcons & 13 different species of bats that live in its talus caves.

| Gateway Arch | February 22, 2018 | Missouri | 192.83 |

The Gateway Arch is a vast 630-foot tall and 630-foot wide monument commemorating Jefferson's Lewis and Clark Expedition and the subsequent westward expansion of the country. On the west side of the arch, you can find the Old Courthouse, which was involved in one of America's most famous court cases - about slavery. An underground museum explains how the arch was built and how America expanded westward.

| Indiana Dunes | February 15, 2019 | Indiana | 15,349.08 |

This was once a national lakeshore, but parts of it are now sandy beaches & tall dunes. It also has grassy prairies, peat bogs, and wetland areas with over 2,000 species of plants and animals.

| White Sands | December 20, 2019 | New Mexico | 146,344.31 |

The Tularosa Basin in southern New Mexico is ringed by mountains and includes the White Sands Missile Range. A 275-square-mile field of white sand dunes composed of gypsum crystals and sitting inside the White Sands Missile Range, this National Park offers visitors some of the world's best opportunities to play in bright, white gypsum sand that reflects all colors.

| New River Gorge | December 27, 2020 | West Virginia | 7,021 |

New River Gorge is the country's deepest gorge east of the Mississippi. The park consists primarily of the lower area around the New River Gorge Bridge, which features some of the best whitewater rafting in North America. The smaller non-contiguous sections in the re-designated stretch of the New River National Wild and Scenic River showcase Thurmond's ghost town, the scenic Grandview vista, and Sandstone Falls. The other 65,165 acres in this area are now designated as a national preserve that runs 53 miles through its course.

Acadia

American Simoa

Arches

Badlands

Big Bend

Biscayne

Black Canyon of the Gunnison

Bryce Canyon

Canyonlands

Capitol Reef

Carlsbad Caverns

Channel Islands

Congaree

Crater Lake

Cuyahoga Valley

Death Valley

Denali

Dry Tortugas

Everglades

Gate of the Arctic

Gateway Arch

Glacier

Glacier Bay

Grand Canyon

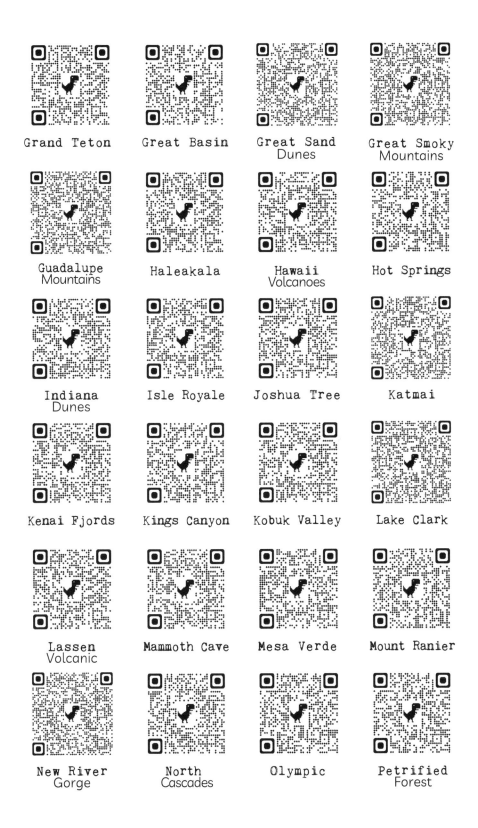

Grand Teton

Great Basin

Great Sand Dunes

Great Smoky Mountains

Guadalupe Mountains

Haleakala

Hawaii Volcanoes

Hot Springs

Indiana Dunes

Isle Royale

Joshua Tree

Katmai

Kenai Fjords

Kings Canyon

Kobuk Valley

Lake Clark

Lassen Volcanic

Mammoth Cave

Mesa Verde

Mount Ranier

New River Gorge

North Cascades

Olympic

Petrified Forest

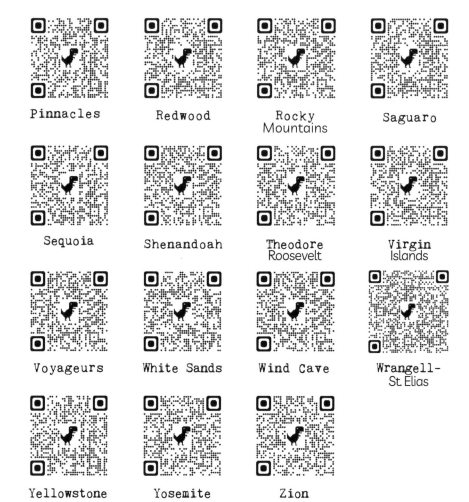

Pinnacles

Redwood

Rocky
Mountains

Saguaro

Sequoia

Shenandoah

Theodore
Roosevelt

Virgin
Islands

Voyageurs

White Sands

Wind Cave

Wrangell-
St. Elias

Yellowstone

Yosemite

Zion

ACADIA
25 Visitor Center Road
Hulls Cove Visitor Center
Bar Harbor, ME 04609
207-288-3338

AMERICAN SAMOA
Pago Pago, AS 96799

684-633-7082 X22

ARCHES
N Hwy 191, Moab,
84532, UT

435-719-2299

BADLANDS
25216 Ben Reifel Road
Interior, SD 57750

605-433-5361

BIG BEND
1 Panther Junction
Big Bend National Park,
TX 79834
432-477-2251

BISCAYNE
9700 SW 328th Street
Sir Lancelot Jones Way
Homestead, FL 33033
305-230-1144

BLACK CANYON OF THE GUNNISON
South Rim Visitor Center
9800 Highway 347
Montrose, CO 81401
970-641-2337 X205

BRYCE CANYON
Highway 63
Bryce Canyon National Park
Bryce, UT 84764
435-834-5322

CANYONLANDS
2282 Resource Blvd.
Moab , UT 84532

435-719-2313

CAPITOL REEF
52 West Headquarters Drive
Torrey, UT 84775
435-425-3791
CARE_INFORMATION@NPS.GOV

CARLSBAD CAVERNS
727 Carlsbad Caverns Highway
Carlsbad, NM 88220

575-785-2232

CHANNEL ISLANDS
1901 Spinnaker Drive
Ventura, CA 93001

805-658-5730

CONGAREE
100 National Park Road
Hopkins, SC 29061

803-776-4396

CRATER LAKE
Crater Lake , OR 97604

541-594-3000

CUYAHOGA VALLEY
6947 Riverview Road
Peninsula, OH 44264

440-717-3890

DEATH VALLEY
California Hwy 190
U.S. Route 95 Nevada

760-786-3200

DENALI
Mile 237 Highway 3
Denali Park, AK 99755

907-683-9532

DRY TORTUGAS
40001 SR-9336
Homestead, FL 33034

305-242-7700

EVERGLADES
40001 State Road-9336
Homestead, FL 33034

305-242-7700

GATES OF THE ARCTIC
101 Dunkel St
Fairbanks, AK 99701

907-459-3730

GATEWAY ARCH
Fourth Street between
Market and Chestnut streets
St. Louis, MO 63102
314-655-1600

GLACIER
64 Grinnell Drive
 Park Headquarters
West Glacier, MT 59936
406-888-7800

GLACIER BAY
1 Park Road
Gustavus, AK 99826

907-697-2230

GRAND CANYON
20 South Entrance Road
Grand Canyon, AZ 86023

928-638-7888

GRAND TETON
103 Headquarters Loop
Moose, WY 83012

307-739-3399

GREAT BASIN
Lehman Caves Visitor Center
Nevada 488
Baker, NV 89311 .

775-234-7331

GREAT SAND DUNES
Visitor Center
11999 State Highway 150
Mosca, CO 81146
719-378-6395

GREAT SMOKY MOUNTAINS
Sugarlands Visitor Center
1420 Little River Road
Gatlinburg, TN 37738
305-242-7700

GUADALUPE MOUNTAINS
400 Pine Canyon
Salt Flat, TX 79847

915-828-3251

HALEAKALA
Haleakala National Park
Makawao , HI 96768

808-572-4400

HAWAII VOLCANOES
1 Crater Rim Drive
Hawaii National Park, HI 96718

808-985-6011

HOT SPRINGS
Fordyce Bathhouse Visitor Cntr
369 Central Avenue
Hot Springs, AR 71901
501-620-6715

INDIANA DUNES
1215 SR-49
Porter, IN 46304

219-395-1882

ISLE ROYALE
Mainland Headquarters
800 East Lakeshore Drive
Houghton, MI 49931
906-482-0984

JOSHUA TREE
74485 National Park Drive
Twentynine Palms,
CA 92277-3597
760-367-5500

KATMAI
1000 Silver Street
Building 603
King Salmon, AK 99613
907-246-3305

KENAI FJORDA

Main Park Visitor Center
Seward Small Boat Harbor
Seward , AK 99664
907-422-0500

NORTH CASCADES

810 State Route 20
Sedro-Woolley, WA 98284

360-854-7200

KINGS CANYON

47050 Generals Highway
Three Rivers, CA 93271

559-565-3341

OLYMPIC

Olympic National Park Visitor Center
3002 Mount Angeles Road
Port Angeles , WA 98362
360-565-3130

KOBUK VALLEY

171 3rd Ave
Kotzebue, AK 99752

907-442-3890

PETRIFIED FOREST

1 Park Road
Petrified Forest, AZ 86028

928-524-6228

LAKE CLARK

Alaska Peninsula
Not located on road system
Port Alsworth, AK 99653
907-644-3626

PINNACLES

5000 East Entrance Road
Paicines, CA 95043

831-389-4486

LASSEN VOLCANIC

38050 Highway 36 East
Park Headquarters
Mineral, CA 96063
530-595-4480

REDWOOD

1111 Second Street
Crescent City, CA 95531

707-464-6101

MAMMOTH CAVES

1 Visitor Center Parkway
Mammoth Cave, KY
           42259-0007
270-758-2180

ROCKY MOUNTAIN

1000 US Hwy 36
Estes Park, CO 80517

970-586-1206

MESA VERDE

Mile .7 Headquarters Loop Road
Mesa Verde National Park,
CO 81330
970-529-4465

SAGUARO

3693 S Old Spanish Trail
Tucson , AZ 85730

520-733-5153

MOUNT RANIER

39000 State Route 706 E,
Ashford, WA 98304

360-569-2211

SEQUOIA

47050 Generals Highway
Three Rivers, CA 93271

559-565-3341

NEW RIVER GORGE

104 Main Street
Glen Jean, WV 25846

304-465-0508

SHENANDOAH

3655 US Hwy. 211 East Luray,
VA 22835-9036

540-999-3500

THEODORE ROOSEVELT
315 Second Avenue
Medora, ND 58645

701-623-4466

WRANGELL--ST ELIAS
Mile 106.8 Richardson Highway
Copper Center , AK 99573

907-822-5234

VIRGIN ISLANDS
1300 Cruz Bay Creek
St. John, VI 00830

340-776-6201 X238

YELLOWSTONE
2 Officers Row
Yellowstone National Park HQ
Yellowstone National Park,
WY 82190   307-344-7381

VOYAGEURS
Voyageurs National Park HQ
360 Hwy 11 East
International Falls, MN 56649
218-283-6600

YOSEMITE
Tioga Rd Hwy 120 & Hwy 140
Yosemite National Park,
CA 95389

209-372-0200

WHITE SANDS
19955 Highway 70 West
Alamogordo, NM 88310

575-479-6124

ZION
1 Zion Park Blvd.
State Route 9
Springdale, UT 84767

435-772-3256

WIND CAVE
26611 US Highway 385
Hot Springs, SD 57747

605-745-4600

Made in the USA
Monee, IL
28 November 2022